Living into God's Dream

Dismantling Racism in America

Edited by Catherine Meeks
Foreword by Jim Wallis

Morehouse Publishing
NEW YORK · HARRISBURG · DENVER

Dedication

To Malissa Alberta Jackson Meeks,
my mother who taught me revolutionary patience.

To Bishop Michael Curry
in appreciation for your courageous leadership.

Unless otherwise noted, the Scripture quotations contained herein are from the New Revised Standard Version Bible, copyright © 1989 by the Division of Christian Education of the National Council of Churches of Christ in the U.S.A. Used by permission. All rights reserved.

Morehouse Publishing, 19 East 34th Street, New York, NY 10016
Morehouse Publishing is an imprint of Church Publishing Incorporated.
www.churchpublishing.org

Cover painting by Roger Hutchison
Cover design by Laurie Klein Westhafer, Bounce Design
Typeset by Denise Hoff

Library of Congress Cataloging-in-Publication Data

A record of this book is available from the Library of Congress.

ISBN-13: 978-0-8192-3321-9 (pbk.)
ISBN-13: 978-0-8192-3322-6 (ebook)

Printed in the United States of America

Contents

Foreword

As I sit down to write the foreword to this timely and urgently needed collection of essays, I can report with a sense of hope that new conversations with commitments to action on racism *are* happening in communities all over the country. Catherine Meeks, the editor of this important volume and my dear friend over many years, was a leader in several of those conversations in Atlanta.

Catherine has been a leader in the struggle for racial justice for a long time, and I am proud to have called myself one of her allies for many years. She has masterfully compiled a deep, probing, and honest collection of essays on how people of faith and conscience of all ethnicities can work together to dismantle racism in America. Her writing, and that of her fellow authors, is moving, thoughtful, and courageous.

In January 2016, I embarked on a "town hall" tour around my latest book, *America's Original Sin: Racism, White Privilege, and the Bridge to a New America.* As someone who has worked on racial justice for the last fifty years—and as someone who has witnessed with dismay the incredibly polarized conversation occurring at the national level—I did not know entirely what to expect.

I strongly believe that truth-telling about America's original sin of devaluing Black and indigenous lives—and the way that sin still lingers in so many of our systems today—must be a multiracial vocation and that the commitment to action that must follow from these conversations must also be multiracial. I had many questions. Are White people ready to hear a call to repent racism and the false idol of whiteness? Will White Christians, in particular, be ready to hear that they are called to be more Christian than White? Will people of color feel safe and empowered to lead and speak honestly about these painful issues in town hall settings?

What I found made me start to feel some hope in our ability to have these difficult, uncomfortable, and necessary conversations. In St. Louis, Chicago, New York, Baltimore, and many other cities, these conversations were *already happening*, and new discussions are emerging and being led by young leaders and activists of all ethnic backgrounds. These powerful experiences have continued in cities all across the country. The most common thing I heard from those who came was that they were "inspired" and "ready to act."

But in spite of this, the task of having these conversations and building a commitment to action toward racial justice and healing in the United States is far from over. So we must continue to go deeper into these transforming questions, and bring them to all corners of our country. Powerful voices of leaders and scholars of color must continue to be lifted up, with honest responses from, as Ta-Nehisi Coates so brilliantly puts it, "those Americans who believe that they are white."[1] With each conversation we must go deeper—gaining new insights, language, and examples from which to draw.

And that's why this collection of essays is so valuable.

Living into God's Dream starts way back in the first chapter of Genesis when God says, "Let us make humankind in our image, according to our likeness" and all of us were created in the image of God. It ends in the seventh chapter of the book of Revelation where all of us, in our own tribes and languages and in all of our rich diversity, are worshipping God together. We are still very much in the midst of the fulfillment of God's dream, but it is deeply satisfying that, even in the face of our pain and struggle, we have seen that dream and believe it will shape the end of human history. This book not only reveals the problems we still face but opens up the changes in hearts, minds, and policies that will take us forward. The essays are both prophetic and practical.

Together, Catherine and her colleagues are proposing real solutions to move us ever closer to the dream of the "Beloved Community" envisioned by Martin Luther King Jr. I am proud to continue standing beside Catherine as we pursue a nation where God's dream can change our lives, our churches, our communities, our nation, and God's world. I hope you will join us.

Jim Wallis
Washington, D.C., June 15, 2016

---

1 Ta-Nehisi Coates, *Between the World and Me* (New York: Spiegel and Grau, 2015), 6.

Introduction

Catherine Meeks

How can African Americans and Whites build a foundation that will allow for honest and fruitful conversation? Is it possible to build enough trust between Blacks and Whites for authentic relationships to develop? What do White people need to consider who want to be conscious about racism and its role in the destruction of African American life in America? What do African Americans need to do now? How can our faith and spiritual journeys inform the work of dismantling racism?

These are some of the questions that frame the conversation being forged within this book. Each contributor is quite clear about the need for a different conversation on race in the twenty-first century than the one held in the twentieth century. But they are equally as clear about the difficulty in trying to discern what that conversation needs to encompass and the challenge surrounding the effort to bring Blacks and Whites together to engage one another in dialogue.

The loud cry that "this is not your mother's civil rights movement" is not lost on us. We know that the times are different, but we know that there are threads in the current struggle that are not that different at all from the ones of the past. The deep need for authentic dialogue continues. Also, there is a need for overt resistance just as fifty years ago when so many courageous warrior men and women took to the streets. At the present time a major challenge offered to any who will dare to engage in active resistance seems to be when and how to enter into the liberation struggle.

Since much appears to have changed and many of the overt structures that made life almost unbearable for Black people are not around, it is easy for Whites to argue that there is no longer a race problem. The song of a "postracial" America was an easy one to sing after the election of President Barack Obama. That notion lasted for a while as the media pundits and others used the term long enough for it to begin to sound as if we had arrived at some new level of freedom in America. But it did not take long for the reality of having a Black family in the White House to sink into the consciousness of many who believe that house is for Whites only and the old virulent racism of the nineteenth and twentieth centuries came to the surface and declared itself alive and well.

There has been no time in the history of America when a president and his family have been treated as this president and his family. The racist comments that have been made about them and the insults to the office are clear evidence of how far we are from being a "postracial" country. The past can no longer take cover in unconsciousness. We have to wake up and realize that it is late and we are many miles from racial equality.

The eight of us who have come together to create this book, *Living into God's Dream: Dismantling Racism in America,* believe that it is possible to look into the mirror to see the truth about ourselves and that we can find the courage and strength to face that truth with the determination to create new and healing narratives about race. We have embraced this task from several perspectives. There are psychological, sociological, and theological threads woven together in this book through personal stories as well as the stories of others who are doing all that they can to forge a new path of genuine racial healing and freedom.

The lead chapter by Dr. Luther Smith calls into the notion that God has a dream for us to be a community and his chapter explores the nature of that dream, what hinders it, and some of the ways that we can begin to embrace it. Dr. Lerita Coleman Brown follows with an enthusiastic assertion that healing the minds of Blacks and Whites alike can lead to the possibility of cultivating the spirit. This is the work that must be done if there is to be true healing. I speak in two chapters about the reasons to continue the conversation on race and the pain that comes to Black parents when their children experience this country as a hard place in which to live because their skin happens not to be white. Don Mosley offers a brilliant analysis of White privilege and its dogged determination to hold him hostage from an early age to his awakening as a young man living and working outside of the United States as a Peace Corps volunteer.

Dr. Diane D'Souza chronicles three stories of groups of people who came together to work on dismantling racism. While these might be viewed as small examples in some ways, they will give the reader courage as well as wonderful ideas about the ways in which the monstrous system of racism can be tackled by a small group of people who set their intention toward destroying it. Dr. Lynn Huber merges her passion and compassion for Palestinians and African Americans in her discussion of the ways that safe spaces can be conceived and built that will make it possible for the Beloved Community to evolve. Bishop Robert C. Wright follows this chapter with an insightful discussion of the ways in which the South is the Holy Land for America. The combination of Scripture, storytelling, and the lyrics of songs and poetry helps to engage the reader in this provocative discussion and illumine the complexities that surround all efforts to understand the southern ethos. Finally, the work which is being done by the Atlanta Episcopal Diocese Beloved Community: Commission for Dismantling Racism is described by Beth King and me. The Commission has evolved from a group of people who were holding rather unproductive monthly meetings and sponsoring dismantling racism training that many people in the diocese spent a fair amount of time thinking of ways to avoid into a highly functioning group. This inspiring story can help to encourage others who are doing similar work.

The major intention of this book is to offer a body of work that is both informative and practical. The chapters can lead the reader to deep reflection about their own journey through America as a White person or as a person of color. Since there is a possibility to read this book in many ways, the hope is that it will be a valuable tool for all who are attempting to have conversations on race and all who are actively seeking to promote racial healing and who are looking for racial justice to grow among us.

This book can be enjoyed by a single reader or a group ready to engage this subject through a diverse lens. It can be used in classrooms, workshops, and in multiple settings where there is an effort to create a dialogue while supporting the notion that this work is ongoing. The work of dismantling racism is most effective when engaged as spiritual formation. It is ongoing in the same way that keeping spiritual disciplines of prayer, silence, and Bible study might be embraced. It requires patience because it cannot be done in a short period of time. It does not matter whether one is orchestrating conversations on race or organizing direct action, it requires patience along with skill and a willingness to move beyond one's zones of comfort.

The eight contributors to this work are people who have spent a significant number of years working to heal ourselves and trying to help others locate the places where healing can occur. We share faith and a commitment to be intentional about racial healing and all of us are clear about the need for all of this work to be located underneath the umbrella of faith and an unwavering commitment to seek healing.

This is a testament to the possibilities that can arrive on the shores of one's life when there is an openness and a willingness to step into the red sea of racism with a little faith and a deep determination to leave this world better than one found it. It makes it clear that the work is not simple, the issues are complicated, and the work, though difficult, is possible. The hope is that all who read this book will be inspired in all of the particular ways that are needed to help them advance the conversation on race and to find the necessary energy, courage, or new insights that can make it possible for them to work to change the racial narrative in America.

Many blessings to every reader.

CHAPTER 1

Living into God's Dream of Community

Luther E. Smith Jr.

Does racism exist in the United States? This question permeates news broadcasts whenever there are public demonstrations about police brutality against Black citizens, or the Supreme Court is deciding cases on voting rights and affirmative action, or economic reports show that Black and Hispanic communities suffer the highest unemployment rates, or graphs indicate the disparity between the number of Black and Hispanic and White high school graduates, or the mass incarceration of Black and Hispanic citizens as compared to White citizens, or reports are released about the epidemic rate of suicides among Native American children.

Often this question about racism results in a slew of questions. What's the difference between racism and prejudice? Are Black and Hispanic people also racists? How strong are the links between current racial problems and historic realities of enslavement, discrimination, and injustice? Does the focus on racism shift attention away from opportunities for self-determination? Is there biological evidence for the concept of race?

These questions merit rigorous engagement. At the same time we must be aware of how asking more questions can be a strategy to avoid answering the prior question and dealing with its challenges: "Does racism exist in the United States?" The answer is "Yes." This is a fact. No amount of complexity or denial or embarrassment about this fact makes it less true.

Two follow-up questions that are a strategic engagement, rather than a strategic avoidance, of racism are: Why does racism continue to persist? And how can we reduce its poisonous impact on society?

Naming Realities

Overcoming deadly forces begins with understanding them. The cancer researcher conducts hundreds of experiments to understand how some cells cause and other cells help to treat cancer. Climate scientists are identifying the major human behaviors that contribute to climate temperature increases that portend catastrophic consequences for all life on earth. And we must have a clear understanding of why racism persists if we hope to engage it effectively.

As I write, there is twenty-four-hour media coverage on Muslims being portrayed as immediate and potential threats to security. Considerable attention is being given to state governors who are refusing to accept Muslim refugees seeking asylum in the United States. However, the rhetoric and many acts of violence against Muslims around the world are also occurring against Muslim citizens of the United States and their mosques. This ethnic and religious bigotry is being headlined as expressions of racism. Critics counter that this inflammatory rhetoric and violent behavior are "un-American."

The critics might be correct if they were only referring to the American *ideal* of respect and equality for all people regardless of race, religion, and ethnicity. The "un-American" label, however, is grossly incorrect when one surveys American history. Enslavement of Africans, broken treaties and wars against Native American Peoples, abuse of Chinese and Mexican immigrant workers, Jim Crow laws, violence against the most recent waves of immigrants, the rallying of lynch mobs against African Americans and Jews, Japanese internment camps, and the mass incarceration industrial complex are all American realities. Racism persists because its oppressive tenets are woven throughout the whole fabric of American history.

Centuries of racial discrimination and injustice are the foundation upon which current social and economic institutions stand. Education, for example, is touted as a way for persons to participate fully in the American dream of opportunity and resourceful living. Schools, however, report major disparities in the educational achievement of Black and Hispanic students when compared to White students. This outcome is not because White babies are born more intelligent than Black and Hispanic babies. Major factors for this disparity are the differences in educational resources for local schools, the impact of poverty on students' ability to have adequate nutrition and a resourceful home environment for study, and the quality of community life for students. Generational patterns of such factors compound the difficulty in overcoming the problems that current students experience. These generational patterns developed in schools and communities that were afflicted by discriminatory housing, employment, and social service policies and practices. Racism is embedded in how American institutions and systems function.

Racism also persists because a large segment of the population benefits from it. This explains why and how individuals perpetuate the system of racism, even without their conscious awareness of the implications of their actions. The existence of racism relies upon it having the personal commitment of some and the inaction of many.

One of the personal commitments to racism occurs with individuals who value their "White privilege" to the extent that they will mount efforts to oppose policies designed to redress current racial inequities caused by the history of racism. Affirmative Action to admit Black and Hispanic students to colleges is considered discrimination against White applicants who are not accepted for admission. Affirmative action to correct historic discrimination in employment practices is interpreted as the violation of the job-seeking rights of White applicants. In both cases, White applicants resist strategies to dismantle racism when the strategies are perceived to diminish their own opportunities to pursue the dreams they have for themselves. A second group that perpetuates racism includes those White persons who believe they are superior to other races. Maintaining definite boundaries between the races is therefore crucial to preserving their superior and rightful standing in society. The self-understanding as superior is so psychologically fulfilling that such persons will even forego economic benefits that would accrue from associating with other races as equals. W. E. B. Du Bois writes about this occurring in his book *Black Reconstruction*. Whiteness served as a "wage" that compensated White workers for the income lost from failing to join with Black laborers to demand higher wages. Historian David R. Roediger comments upon Du Bois's analysis in his book *The Wages of Whiteness: Race and the Making of the American Working Class*:

> Race feeling and the benefits conferred by whiteness made white Southern workers forget their "practically identical interests" with the Black poor and

accept stunted lives for themselves and for those more oppressed than themselves. . . . Du Bois held that this would have been a better and more class-conscious nation and world had the heritage of slavery and racism not led the working class to prize whiteness.[1]

Identifying as White can be so fundamental to feeling properly located in the best racial group that "the American ideal" of all persons being created equal is no more than a platitude to explain the superior abilities of those who have risen to the top. A third group unapologetically declares itself to not only be superior to other races, it is active in advocating for racial segregation and even terrorism against other races. Periodically the activities of a few of these groups will surface in the news. The Southern Poverty Law Center's work, however, indicates that hundreds of these groups are pervasive throughout the United States and that their espousal of racism is relentless through rallies, magazine publications, and the various media of the Internet. The fourth group is persons who are actually appalled by racism. However, they are so bewildered by its scope and frightened by possible conflicts arising from their involvement in efforts to dismantle racism that they keep their distance from any kind of activism against racism. This is not only the largest group, it is probably larger than the three other groups combined. Opposing racism but not being active in combatting it sounds rather benign—especially when compared to the attitudes and activism of the first three groups. Forfeiting opportunities to act creatively for race relations may be the greatest contributor to racism's malignant persistence in society. I believe Rabbi Abraham Joshua Heschel was right when he said: "In a free society, some are guilty, but all are responsible."[2] All of us are responsible for the persistence of racism. The failure to be involved in addressing racism is also to be guilty of perpetuating it.

The systemic realities of racism are not immutable. They increase or diminish by the extent of personal and collective involvement we give to combat racism. Individuals giving their hearts to dismantling racism are key to reducing its horrific blight on life. The transformations of hearts alone will not undo racism. Racism is embedded in our institutions. Still, *the transformation of hearts is essential to participating in the interpersonal and political processes that result in the transformation of racist systems.*

---

1 David R. Roediger, *The Wages of Whiteness: Race and the Making of the American Working Class* (New York: Verso, 2007), 13.

2 https://en.wikiquote.org/wiki/Abraham_Joshua_Heschel

Casting Our Eyes to the Vision

Giving our hearts to dismantling racism is a calling and a challenge worthy of us. Christian commitment, however, should never have *being against* evil as its ultimate focus. If our faith is reduced to only being against evil, then evil consumes our attention and energies. We then have a perverted devotion to evil—a devotion driven by outrage.

The Christian faith is based upon *being committed to* God's dream for us personally and communally. Our living creatively into the future involves our devotion to *the compelling vision* of God's realm of shalom. This is a major biblical theme in Judaism and Christianity. Throughout the sacred Scriptures, God is longing for a people who will become a faithful community of witness to God's commandments and love. The faithful community, in covenant relationship with God, is integral to God's purposes that the whole creation be in harmony with God.

Racism is a social and spiritual crisis. Being motivated *against* racism is to recognize a major impediment to the realization of this Beloved Community. However, eliminating racism does not, in and of itself, bring forth Beloved Community. Other societal ills are soul crushing. Living in community can be experienced as "hell on earth" when society fails to give sufficient attention to addressing poverty, mental health care, religious bigotry that pits one religion against another, sexism, violence as a chosen remedy to conflict, and hostilities against people because of their sexual orientation. Opposing racism and other social ills need to be rooted in the vision of God's dream of Beloved Community where persons respect, nurture, and love one another as sacred people of God.

The primary significance of this vision to living the Christian faith is recorded in Luke's Gospel when a lawyer stands to test Jesus and asks: "Teacher, what must I do to inherit eternal life?" Jesus responds, "What is written in the law? What do you read there?" And the lawyer answers, "You shall love the Lord your God with all your heart, and with all your soul, and with all your strength, and with all your mind; and your neighbor as yourself." And then Jesus says to the lawyer, "You have given the right answer; do this, and you will live." The lawyer decides to press Jesus on how far this love-ethic extends to others, so he asks a question that shines a light on his assumption that some criteria must be operative to determine who does and does not merit this extravagant love. He asks, "And who is my neighbor?" Jesus proceeds to tell him a story about a traveler being brutally assaulted by criminals and left in a critical condition. When persons who were part of the victim's own religious identity saw him, they had excuses to avoid responding to the man's needs. Then a Samaritan, someone whose religion was generally considered despicable, came by and upon seeing the man gave him immediate and longer-term care. Jesus then asks the lawyer, "Which of these three, do you think, was a neighbor to the man who fell into the hands of the robbers?" The lawyer identifies the Samaritan. Jesus tells the lawyer to continue life by showing this extravagant love to others—even those we think of as being outside the circle of our caring relationships.[3]

This vision and ethic of loving neighbors inspires our commitment to overcome racism. At the same time, the message's simplicity can be disturbing because it eviscerates the excuse that racism is too complicated for personal involvement. Everyone has the opportunity and capacity to act as a neighbor. The message is also disturbing because it compels us to go beyond the homogeneous relational boundaries we have constructed.

In this parable, Jesus not only gives us a command, "Go and do likewise," he provides us a method for honoring what God dreams for us. We are to love God and love our neighbors. The current reality of alienation from neighbors can be overcome through love. We should be heartened in knowing the power of love to overcome obstacles to the community-making purpose of love. And our hearts should rejoice in knowing the assurance of Jesus that in giving ourselves to loving in this way, we "will live." (Luke 10:28).

Howard Thurman: Mentor for Transformation

Howard Thurman's prophetic witness in overcoming racial barriers is a resource for addressing the challenges of racism to Beloved Community. Thurman played a major role in casting a vision of community that is characterized by justice, peace, and a love-ethic that extends to all persons. In addition to the vision, he was a prophetic worker on behalf of *a process* for community that asserted the power of nonviolent conflict resolution. His work informed the thinking of Martin Luther King Jr. to such an extent that King listed Thurman as one of the ten most influential persons of the twentieth century.[4]

In 1936 Howard Thurman was the first African American to meet with Mohandas K. Gandhi. His conversation with Gandhi received national attention as the basis for creating a movement to overcome racial

---

3   See Luke 10:25–37.

4   King's estimate of Thurman was on a note displayed in an exhibit of the Martin Luther King Jr. Papers Project at Morehouse College.

injustice in the United States.[5] His 1944 cofounding of the first interracial and intercultural church (named "The Church for the Fellowship of All Peoples"; also known as "Fellowship Church"), in both membership and leadership, in the United States was a pioneering accomplishment to demonstrate the church's capacity to overcome the racial divisions of society. This breakthrough inspired others to establish multi-racial and multi-cultural congregations.[6]

The underlying methodology of Thurman's witness to overcome racial alienation and hostility is presented in his book, *Jesus and the Disinherited*. Thurman writes about Jesus's liberating message "to those who stand with their backs against the wall."[7] He interprets Jesus's status as a poor, oppressed Jew as being analogous to the status and plight of African Americans. He then identifies "hate" as a powerful emotion and motivation that pervades society and prevents people from experiencing one another as sisters and brothers.

Thurman concludes that hate begins "in a situation in which there is contact without fellowship, contact that is devoid of any of the primary overtures of warmth and fellow-feeling and genuineness." Next, "contacts without fellowship tend to express themselves in the kind of understanding that is strikingly unsympathetic. There is understanding of a kind, but it is without the healing and reinforcement of personality." Third, "an unsympathetic understanding tends to express itself in the active functioning of ill will." And fourth, "ill will, when dramatized in a human being, becomes hatred walking on the earth." This four-phase development of hate serves as both analysis and basis for a healing prescription.[8]

Physical proximity to one another can provide diverse peoples opportunities for caring relationship. However, without sustained interaction and expressions of intimacy among people of different identities, the stage is set for dramas in which hate will be a leading character. Proximity without a process that forms caring relationships is a deadly combination.

---

5 Also attending this meeting with Gandhi were Sue Bailey Thurman (his wife) and Rev. Edward G. Carroll. For a comprehensive examination of Thurman's meeting with Gandhi, see Quinton Dixie and Peter Eisenstadt, *Visions of a Better World: Howard Thurman's Pilgrimage to India and the Origins of African American Nonviolence* (Boston: Beacon Press, 2011).

6 See Howard Thurman, *Footprints of a Dream: The Story of the Church for the Fellowship of All Peoples* (New York: Harper & Brothers, 1959).

7 Howard Thurman, *Jesus and the Disinherited* (Boston: Beacon Press, 1996), 108. The book was selected as one of thirty texts that have significantly influenced Christian spiritual formation; see Arthur Holder, ed., *Christian Spirituality: The Classics* (New York: Routledge, 2010).

8 Thurman, *Jesus and the Disinherited*, 75–78.

Thurman believes that Jesus's love-ethic was the transforming power for liberating the disinherited from the moribund consequences of hatred. In this love-ethic "every man is potentially every other man's neighbor. Neighborliness is nonspatial; it is qualitative. A man must love his neighbor directly, clearly, permitting no barriers between."[9]

His conclusions about love and nurturing relationships guided his ministry throughout his life. In his autobiography, *With Head and Heart*, he wrote: "Meaningful and creative experiences between peoples can be more compelling than all the ideas, concepts, faiths, fears, ideologies, and prejudices that divide them; and [I have] absolute faith that if such experiences can be multiplied and sustained over a time interval of sufficient duration *any* barrier that separates one person from another can be undermined and eliminated."[10]

When Thurman speaks of eliminating the barriers that separate people, he is not meaning that differences in race, religion, and ethnicity are to be dismissed or considered inconsequential. In and of themselves, these differences are not barriers. They become barriers when they are given interpretations that create hierarchical and dominating relationships.

Rather than attempting to establish a community where differences have no standing, Thurman's success at Fellowship Church and other places was based on forming reconciling communities where differences were acknowledged and celebrated. His reconciling process for people of diverse backgrounds involved establishing respectful relationships that pursue understanding through experiences of connecting with one another. Such transformational experiences involve listening, risking vulnerability, making the commitment to meet for an extended period of time, identifying common ground, celebrating distinctions, and cultivating compassion. Thurman is convinced that the reconciling process is "more compelling" and more effective in leading people to God's vision of human community than projects that begin and end by idolizing differences.[11]

---

9 Ibid., 89.

10 Howard Thurman, *With Head and Heart: The Autobiography of Howard Thurman* (New York: Harcourt Brace and Company, 1979), 148.

11 Thurman's conviction has the same principles as Contact Theory developed by Gordon Allport—a theory that has been used by social psychologists, sociologists, and political scientists to explain important conditions for overcoming prejudice and conflict between individuals and groups. However, Thurman put forth his principles two decades *before* Allport's groundbreaking work *The Nature of Prejudice* (1954).

What Must We Do to Inherit God's Dream of Community?

Howard Thurman provides us keen insights for taking personal responsibility and opportunities to combat racism. His analysis of hate beginning in situations of no contact and no sympathetic understanding focuses on the crisis of alienation. After becoming aware of who are our neighbors, we are faced with the question: How do we bridge the gap of alienation with our neighbors?

The opportunities to end racial alienation are available. Sometimes the opportunity involves volunteering for a community service program where people of a different race are present. Some of these people may be recipients of services to develop literacy skills, or exercise, or to cultivate home maintenance skills. Others who bring racial diversity into your life may be staff or volunteers themselves. Most important is the realization that bridging the racial divide is more than showing up and providing a service. What is needed is the commitment to give sufficient time to cultivate and sustain relationships, as Thurman says, of "sympathetic understanding." The heart given in vulnerability, trust, and caring must accompany whatever energies are spent to complete projects.

When the heart is offered in this way, presence with one another is not characterized by a server/recipient relationship. Instead, a mutual exchange of gifts occurs as the depths of hearts are offered and experienced.

Sometimes the opportunity to bridge racial alienation comes by way of invitation. What may seem like only a courtesy invitation into another's church, or social event, or lunchtime meal, or convalescent home could lead to the transforming experience of living in another's heart. This is one reason that invitations should never be received with the attitude that a "yes" or "no" is inconsequential. Invitations can be life altering for all involved.

Knowing this, how do you extend invitations to and accept invitations from persons of a different race? How do you envision inviting others to a meal or a special event in your life so that your heart expands as you hold dear their heritage and personal histories? What environments best enable persons to pursue a path of friendship?

One of the oldest meanings of the word "reconciliation" is "a place of meeting." This stresses that overcoming alienation requires coming together. If we are to deepen understanding so that processes of reconciliation might begin, we must establish and come together in public and private places.

This emphasis on being present and interactive with one another reminds us that we cannot approach the overcoming alienation only by reading books or viewing documentaries about race and racism. When people have not had relationships with persons from another racial group, their understanding is impersonal. Knowledge about another is then formed through positive and negative impressions based on reports. The knowledge may be laudatory of another race; still it fails to capture a deeper knowing that comes from sustained interpersonal communication—a knowing that is fundamental to personal and systemic transformation.

Years ago I led a workshop on race relations at a local church. After my presentation, a White man stood to give his testimony about how his own racial consciousness was formed. He said: "I am so grateful that I had parents who taught me to be respectful of all people, and that I was not to think of myself as superior to others. As a White boy growing up in the South, they made certain that I valued and loved all people. And I can honestly say that I grew up through adolescence loving all Black people." He paused and continued, "Then I finally met a Black person." The room erupted in laughter immediately and continued throughout his ongoing description of the conflict that ensued in the relationship with this *first* Black man he met.

His "loving all Black people" was a feeling without the content of experience. Until his first meeting with a Black person, Black people were an abstraction. He had embraced the idea of loving Black people, but it was an emotion for the cardboard figures he had imagined Black people to be. Remote affirmation is not a credible substitute for experiences of relationship that hold the promise for in-depth understanding and authentic love.

Interracial relationships can run the spectrum of feelings that are found in all relationships. People of different races can be truly at home with one another and delight in the ease of conversations and readiness to care. People of different races can also be tense together with defenses up because of mistrust and perhaps even hostility from wounds suffered in previous interracial encounters. The song's refrain "the more we get together, the happier we'll be" is not true for many experiences of people crossing racial boundaries.

Churches committed to overcoming racism will need to be sensitive to the diverse experiences and feelings that may exist in an interracial gathering. Some processes of coming together may flow easily as persons offer their histories and hopes. Other situations may require a skilled facilitator to help persons to speak and hear fears, anger, guilt, yearning, and other emotions from lives lived in interracial conflict and/or interracial alienation. Bridging the gap of racial alienation can be joyful and it can be painful. Sometimes the joy and the pain occur within the same people involved in crossing the racial divide.

What can be said with certainty is that cultivating creative race relations is a lifelong process. This is not a matter of completing what needs to be done in a series of workshops or Lenten study group sessions. There are no quick fixes. In fact, "fixing" race relations is not the goal. We do not fix one another. Every person has a depth of being and becoming that is dynamic. It should be honored. There may be dimensions of the person that require healing. But the notion of fixing someone or a relationship violates the very character of what it means to be human beings.

Correspondingly, racial reconciliation is not an outcome that marks the end to racial conflict. Racial issues are too dynamic, complex, and evolving to be fixed once and for all. I believe a more significant and accurate term for overcoming racial alienation is *being active in reconciling processes*. Being in the reconciling process places us in the relationships and places and times where faith, hope, and love abide. The reconciling process is a destination worthy of Christian commitment.

We Can Do This

Earlier, this chapter listed ways some people experience privilege from racism. Also true is the fact that everyone suffers from it. The byproducts of racism are toxic for an environment in which everyone breathes. Denied housing, jobs, and educational opportunities for generations, whole communities experience futility and its consequences of crime and despair. Law enforcement's too frequent harassment and violence against Black and Hispanic citizens have undermined the respect needed from all citizens for effective policing. Mass incarceration and the dehumanizing conditions of prisons have made the nation less safe for everyone. Racial alienation fuels stereotypes and mistrust that result in fear and hostility. We are all in this together.

Yes, everyone suffers the effects of racism. However, our greatest inspiration for personal and systemic change hopefully comes from anticipating the joy of living in God's dream of community. God dreams of community where we love one another as neighbors with all our heart, soul, strength, and mind. Living as caring neighbors is not a reality beyond time and place. God calls us to live now into this dream for community.

The above-mentioned personal initiatives may seem inadequate to impact the complex and often impersonal institutions and systems that perpetuate racism. Again, I am not proposing *the plan* that will strike the deathblow to racism. Personal initiatives to overcome racial alienation, however, are essential for involving persons in dismantling racist policies, practices, and mindsets. We must never accept the conclusion that institutions and systems are beyond the capacity of individuals (personally and collectively) to change them. Such a conclusion is advanced to discourage efforts intent on social transformation. This is the defeatist conclusion of especially two types of persons: 1) those who are so benefiting from the status quo that they want to defend and perpetuate systems of the status quo; and 2) those who are so unnerved by the demands of long-term struggle that they declare defeat rather than enter the fray.

Institutions and systems are conceived and protected by individuals. They thrive and fail because of human involvement. And regardless of how slowly they seem to respond to human intervention, they are susceptible to being reconceived and changed by the determination of those whose vision inspires their ultimate commitments.

Perhaps the greatest challenge for effecting social change has less to do with the power of racist systems than it is about our refusal to significantly alter the priorities of our lives. To break from life rhythms dictated by careers, family obligations, and social circles that make heavy time and energy demands on us is a challenge. We are often captive to routines of association that were established earlier in life. We find it severely difficult to commit time to establish new cross-racial relationships even if we intellectually appreciate the vision of community that can emerge from such relationships. We feel trapped by responsibilities and routines that seem to prevent opportunities to form new relationships. Therefore, working on behalf of Beloved Community becomes a dream deferred.

Perhaps such a devotion to our habits, that also have a stranglehold on our spirits, led Howard Thurman to assert that *religion might be the only hope for a world torn apart by hate and violence.* When family obligations, tribal identities, and career demands provide ample justification to not venture into the added demands of interracial relationships, the desire to submit to God's dream for us may enable us to escape the captivity of the familiar and risk establishing relationships that expand our hearts. With God, we always have a choice. God does not coerce us. We can capitulate to our fears and familiar habits. Or we can choose to live into God's dream of community. I pray that we choose wisely.

2 # Dissecting Racism: Healing Minds, Cultivating Spirits

Lerita Coleman Brown

> *Our young must be taught that racial peculiarities do*
> *exist, but that beneath the skin,*
> *beyond the differing features, and into the true heart*
> *of being,*
> *fundamentally, we are more alike, my friend, than we*
> *are unalike.*
>
> —Maya Angelou

Introduction

Most people are unaware that racial categories and the identities that emerge from them are socially constructed. Infants do not arrive in the world knowing they belong to any racial group. They must *learn* that they are Black or White. They are equally ignorant about their spiritual natures. Yet as human beings begin to acknowledge themselves as spirits, eventually they must admit that everyone else is a spirit as well. Perhaps, then, the dismantling of racism resides in the process of unlearning some false notions about race, and learning some truths about spirituality. Arriving at this intersection, however, may require the correction of misperceptions, restructuring of self-concepts, practicing an enormous amount of forgiveness, and healing old, deep hurts and wounds.

Therefore, this chapter challenges the essentialism of race, of

Blackness and Whiteness in particular, that most people accept as true. Perceptions (frequently fueled by stereotypes) and meanings about racial categories prevent the acknowledgement of a requisite interdependence. However, the domain of spirituality highlights interconnections and is often where racial reconciliation flourishes. Typically settings such as retreat centers and contemplative or listening prayer groups frequently emphasize the commonalities rather than the differences among people.

What did you learn about race as a child? How has your thinking changed and what led to the shift? What role, if any, has spiritual formation played in the transformation of your perceptions and feelings about race? Such questions may stimulate a shift in thinking, a change in heart, and provide rich sustenance for individual or group reflection about dismantling racism.

The Dilemma

At age six, I entered St. Andrew's Catholic school in Pasadena, California. It was the late 1950s and St. Andrew's was a racially integrated as opposed to a racially desegregated school. The only criterion for admission was that one parent be Catholic. At St. Andrews, I became best friends with Karen Gallo, whose affluent family lived in a beautiful home near the Rose Bowl. Karen and I enjoyed running and playing all sorts of games on the playground and soon we asked our mothers if we could spend some time together on Saturdays. I visited Karen first in her large five bedroom home with a huge kitchen, family room, swimming pool, and, to my great shock, a Negro maid. I felt tension as the maid and I eyed each other during that initial visit. Then Karen visited me and my family in our much smaller two expanded to three bedrooms with one bathroom home in our predominantly Negro neighborhood. At age six I couldn't quite discern the social consequences that our differing living situations might engender so I continued to happily cultivate my relationship with Karen. Then Karen suggested an overnight stay. Parents consulted each other and soon I packed up a few items to share a sleepover in Karen's bedroom equipped with bunk beds. Next it was my turn to ask Karen to stay overnight. Then it seemed like time froze. Somehow Karen's parents would not permit her to stay overnight and no matter how my parents tried to explain it to me, I never quite understood what the problem was. Could it be that our house was too small, or that we only had one bathroom instead of four? Was it because we didn't have a Negro maid? Maybe it was because I didn't have bunk beds like Karen had in her room. With two brothers, I possessed my own room with a double bed. Sadly, I sat pondering all of those things in my room during moments of solitude. This incident among others I encountered as I entered the larger social world of school would be my introduction to the complicated world of race relations in America.

Clearly, if I had been living in another state or region of the country, I wouldn't have been attending school with Karen. No matter where I lived, though, sooner or later I was going to be confronted with some event that would let me know my standing as a young Negro girl. Even though Karen and I shared an "equal" world in Catholic school, that same equality did not exist in the world we lived in outside of the classroom. Thus, I concluded from this early occurrence that perhaps something was *wrong with me* or my family, or my skin color. But why? Although my child mind could process that there were indeed different kinds of people—Whites, Blacks, Mexicans, Filipinos, Catholic children of many hues—I couldn't quite grasp why individuals from these groups would be viewed or treated differently. The nuns taught us that God loved each and every one of us the same, so what was the issue? Later I discovered that there was nothing wrong with me, for the difficulty was not with me but out there—in the perceptions of others, perceptions that shaped the social and cultural milieu of the United States.

However, I believe these early experiences affected my self-concept, particularly my racial identity. They shaped my psychological life, a mental world that also sprung from my family history, as well as the political, social, and racial Zeitgeist. This identity shaped by the attitudes and actions of my parents, extended family, teachers, ministers, and the larger social environment of racism is one aspect of this tale.

White Surprise and More

Recently my husband and I found ourselves as the only Black couple on a sea and land tour to Alaska and northern Canada. As retirees of the US government and academia respectively, we were quite accustomed to being "the only ones," meaning being the only people of color in meetings, talks, and conferences. Yet what emerged as most unnerving and tiring were the responses we received from our nearly all White tour group. Many attempted to mask their *surprise* that we are two obviously middle- or upper-middle-class people with LL Bean and Orvis outerwear to signal that. It didn't help that my husband, Warren, carried along a very expensive camera and took photos at nearly every stop.

Within hours our White travel companions clamored to inquire about our occupations and could not hide the shock on their faces when they discovered that Warren, a retired marine biologist, and I, a former psychology professor, loved adventurous travel. I sensed a certain unease set in as they became aware that Warren and I might actually possess a higher socioeconomic status than some of them. The country had witnessed many years of President Barack and First Lady Michelle Obama, a very high profile, upper-middle-class Black couple with impressive academic pedigrees, but to our White travel companions they must be an anomaly, right? I didn't focus long on the personal and social discomfort of my travel companions because I had witnessed it countless times. Yet such social encounters represent rarely publicly discussed assumptions. Americans don't just perceive racial categories but assign value to them. Euro Americans (White people) are valued more highly and assumed to be inherently better (superior) to African Americans (Black people) and most people of color regardless of socioeconomic or educational status. These suppositions undergird most interracial interactions and we unwittingly teach these assumptions to *all* children who in turn internalize them.[1]

In the fifty years that separate these two personal encounters with racism, I sought many explanations. Fortunately, my research on stigma, identity, and self-concept provided me with numerous leads. The knowledge and tools I acquired navigating through over thirty years of college teaching, research, and personal experiences helped to frame my ideas about racism and to consider if it is possible to "dismantle" it. I share this journey now.

Racism—A Working Definition

First I would like to proffer my working definition of racism. This is not a scientific explanation or even a current academic one but based solely on my observations. For me, racism occurs anytime anyone with their thoughts, feelings, or behavior attempts to confine or restrict the inherent potential of another individual based on the attributes associated with his or her phenotype or assumed race or ethnic category. Communication is extremely powerful and shapes identity and self-concept. However, how we communicate to each other is often based on our stereotypes or expectations about one's racial or ethnic group membership. It is rare indeed that our verbal and nonverbal communication is directed to a

---

1 Debby Irving, *Waking Up White, and Finding Myself in the Story of Race* (Cambridge, MA: Elephant Room Press, 2014).

unique person whose life history and experiences are unknown to us. Using this definition and as an example, as an unadulterated racist I would expect each person I meet who *appears* to be Muslim to be a terrorist, each Black to be unintelligent and/or poor, all Whites to be racist, and any Latino to be an illegal alien and I would react accordingly.

I am certain many people would challenge this definition of racism because it is often argued that people who do not hold power and domination can only be prejudiced but not racist. In my estimation, however, there is tremendous power in the psychological impact verbal and nonverbal communication play in the development of identity, self-concept, and social reality. Sociologists would posit that our identities and self-concept arise out of social interactions as we learn to define who we are from others. People internalized a great deal about "who they think they are" from how and what people communicate to them. Stereotypical and deprecatory verbal and nonverbal communication can cripple individuals and their children for generations. Thus identity and self-concept may be the link, the missing puzzle piece to understanding the origins as well as the maintenance of racism.

Moments of Racial Harmony

Attending a desegregated high school in Pasadena, California, in the late 1960s, a result of the suit based on the Brown vs. Board of Education 1954 Supreme Court decision, my class reflected a rainbow coalition of sorts. In addition to the White and Black students that the suit addressed, I attended classes with Mexicans, Filipinos, Japanese, Chinese, Jewish, and Native American Indian students among others. Evidence of racism was more incidental as I could name only a few times in which I felt teachers or counselors favored White students. Unequal education was more attached to socioeconomic status (SES) whereby most of the students in my AP classes were from middle- or upper-class families regardless of race or ethnicity. These adolescent experiences helped me to know that people of all races and ethnicities could peacefully coexist and work together. However, it did not prepare me well for my entry into the University of California system that contained more insidious and often chilling forms of racism.

Trying to Make Sense Out of the Nonsensical

Being a member of a very small group of Black students to enter the University of California, Santa Cruz, in the early 1970s served both as a blessing and a curse. Fortunately, I was admitted with a California State Scholarship to a very popular campus. Yet the reactions I received from students and professors alike were based on the assumption that I didn't meet the admissions requirements. Many White people either acted surprised or labeled me an Equal Opportunity Program (EOP) student and dismissed me. After having such a Kumbaya high school experience, I felt devastated by the rude and crude ways some professors treated me and my academic work. I expected more civilized behavior from more educated Whites. Yet, I also discovered a few compassionate Black and White professors who mentored and provided me with resources to cultivate my budding intellectual acumen. I loved to read, exchange ideas, critically analyze material, and discuss all kinds of topics like philosophy, psychology, Black studies, religious studies, history of consciousness, biology, and world events. My experiences as a Black student desegregating a predominantly White university motivated me to understand why so many White people stared, labeled, stereotyped, denigrated me, and acted like I was an alien on "their" campus while a much smaller minority embraced me. What was the root cause of these differing behaviors?

The Graduate Years—Learning More about Stereotyping

In the early to mid-1970s, studies on attitudes, origins of prejudice, and national surveys on race relations permeated the field of psychology. Soon after I began a social psychology graduate program, the emphasis in the field shifted from investigating how people (mostly White college sophomores) felt toward members of differing races to the cognitive processes underlying racial stereotyping and discrimination.

At first I didn't quite understand the work on social cognition, which suggested that categorizing people who are different is natural because humans classify stimuli all day. These cognitive theories argued classifications are necessary, a part of evolution, a way to discern good vs. evil people as a means of survival. What seemed lacking in these theoretical formulations was any understanding about why categorization morphed into denigration or when the animus emerged, why the hatred manifested. I couldn't resolve the contradiction of White's discriminatory behavior with Blacks in public accommodations while hiring the same people to care and nurture their precious children. And what accounted for the hostility and rage I witnessed during the civil rights movement and in the daily microaggressions I and family members or friends could easily recount? Was it really only fear of change?

In addition, I noticed that constructs like identity, particularly the construction of racial identity of White people, was missing from the cognitive work on stereotyping and even current work on the links between neuroscience and implicit racial biases. It was as if there was some avoidance of a deep examination of the people perpetrating hatred, people engaging in many forms of dehumanization.

I also discovered that so many of the racial stereotypes people hold are mere projections. Each time I encountered the stereotype "lazy and shiftless" associated with Blacks, I wondered where this label originated given its application to a group of people enslaved and imported to this country to work. Weren't the ones watching them labor in the hot fields and in the house the lazy and shiftless ones? Likewise when Dylann Roof recently murdered nine people in a Charleston church, he claimed it was because Blacks are "stupid and violent." Clearly these labels reflected his assessment of himself projected onto innocent people sitting in a prayer group. Thus, I felt solving the racism puzzle involved uncovering what fueled stereotypes, projections, fear, hate, the formation of racial identities, and the intrapsychological push toward separation rather than connection.

Discovering the Construct: Master Status

As a social psychologist viewing social life from a psychological perspective, I noticed many others investigating these same issues through the lens of sociology. Sociological social psychology focuses on how society and social norms mold individuals, identity, and self-concept and how processes like stigma and "othering" develop. Labeling theory, for example, initially described how people mark and stigmatize "deviants" in society. This work evolved into ethnographic studies of stigma and gave birth to another relevant term "master status."[2]

Being Black is stigmatized in the United States and many other places. This means that people who *phenotypically* appear to be Black, or a person of African descent, are devalued and denigrated. Thus, non-Blacks frequently use racial category as the sole attribute or *master status*, thereby discrediting Blacks as individuals who occupy a multitude of other roles (e.g., SES, occupational, political). For many Whites,

---

2 Erving Goffman, *Stigma: Notes on the Management of Spoiled Identity* (Englewood Cliffs, NJ: Prentice-Hall, 1963).

when they encounter a Black person, all they perceive is a *Black* person—
not a doctor, teacher, or astronaut. Writers become Black writers, artists
are categorized by race, even President Obama is considered by some to
be a *Black* president. Thus, due to the use of a master status in interracial interactions, the intelligence and competence of Blacks, no matter
what they achieve in society, are constantly under scrutiny; their competence questioned at every turn. Many Blacks as a result internalize this
stigma and it becomes part of their self-concept. Master status, a learned
behavior, is key to maintaining racism.

Other Concepts: Self-Referencing and Othering

As my career teaching in predominantly White institutions evolved, my
feelings of being an outcast grew stronger. I wondered why my professional experiences differed so much from my high school years. I continued to explore and write about how we learn to stigmatize people
through self-referencing.[3] Most parents do not explicitly teach their children to hate certain groups of people based on their race, religion, or
ethnicity. However, they actively influence the development of implicit
racial biases. Wendell Berry offers a revealing description:

> If a person is lovable and respectable, a child will love or
> respect him without first asking his class or his race or
> his income.[4]

Small children are curious about differences but look to their parents
or caretakers about how to react. If Mom or Dad suddenly tenses up,
grabs their hands in fear, or crosses the street every time they encounter
a Black person, particularly a male, young children learn to *fear* Black
males. Or if young White boys or girls grow up with low self-esteem due
to their educational or economic background, they may be taught (often
by family members or their communities) to displace their negative feelings about their lack of self-worth onto Blacks or members of nonwhite
ethnic groups.

These reactions also aid in the formation and maintenance of in-
groups and out-groups. Learning about how social (racial or ethnic) group
membership originates and operates; forming in-group and out-group

---

3 Lerita Coleman Brown, "Stigma: An Enigma Demystified." Reprinted in *The Disability
Studies Reader, 4th Edition,* ed. Leonard Davis (New York: Routledge, 2013), 139–52.

4 Wendell Berry, *The Hidden Wound* (San Francisco, CA: North Point Press, 1989), 59.

biases helped to explain another sociological phenomenon, "othering." Could this same construct explain why I felt I never quite belonged with my White colleagues? In the case of majority and minority groups, usually the dominant group sets the terms for who is in and who is out. Amy Irving writes about how as a White person she discovered this same phenomenon in her social interactions.

> White skin can erroneously bring high expectations and the message "You belong"; dark skin can erroneously bring low expectations and the message "You don't belong."[5]

Thus, in situations where I was the only Black, "the only one," feeling like an outsider in a group of all Whites permeated my consciousness. By virtue of how interactions were structured or the nature of comments, I always felt like the "other" in the group.

Sociologists also believe that constructs like race and in- and out-groups arise from the othering process. In fact, there are many definitions and worth of social groups that seem natural or essential but emerge from otherness. More common examples are: Woman is the other to man (i.e., being a man means being inherently better than a woman); poor is the other to rich (being rich means being inherently better than someone who is poor); Black is the other to White (i.e., being White means being inherently better than someone who is Black). Many social identities are relational—suggesting that one category lacks meaning without the other. Andrew Okolie eloquently describes it this way:

> Social identities are relational; groups typically define themselves in relation to others. This is because identity has little meaning without the "other." So, by defining itself a group defines others. Identity is rarely claimed or assigned for its own sake. These definitions of self and others have purposes and consequences. They are tied to rewards and punishment, which may be material or symbolic. There is usually an expectation of gain or loss as a consequence of identity claims. This is why identities are contested. Power is implicated here, and because groups do not have equal powers to define both self and

---

5 Irving, *Waking Up White*, 14.

the other, the consequences reflect these power differentials. Often notions of superiority and inferiority are embedded in particular identities.[6]

Horrible instances of "othering" fueled murder during the Holocaust, in Rwanda, and other situations of "ethnic cleansing."[7]

Othering and the Origins of Relational Racial Identities

Many years ago, M. M. Slaughter wrote an intriguing paper, "The Multicultural Self," outlining the differences between White and Black identity and other ethnic identities.[8] Slaughter suggested "society" or the "state," as she terms it, is a major constructor and perpetuator of differences. Thus, social constructs like Black and White often thought of as essential—definite, unchangeable, and true—may not be.

Slaughter begins by noting that individuals lack control over the construction of their racial identities,because they are based on phenotype. Individuals are *raced* by society and this is conveyed in the ways people respond to and communicate with them. Slaughter also labels some cultural or ethnic identities ones of "nomos" because they are embedded in language, food, religious rituals, traditions, or holidays. Within the United States, Native American/American Indian culture serves as a prime example and some Latino and Asian cultural identities fit the criteria as well. However, White and Black identities are labeled identities of absence because the definition of one is based on the other. Hence, although there are historical and political events related to these two identities, there is no real distinct language, food, or religious holidays associated with them in the United States. In essence, a person develops a "White" identity because he or she is not Black and likewise, many aspects of Black identity initially are determined by one's sense that they are "not White." As noted earlier, Black is the "other" for White and vice versa. However, because the "universal human being" is thought to be a White, middle-class, heterosexual, able-bodied man, Whites rarely feel

6　Andrew Okolie cited in Zuleyka Zevallos, "What Is Otherness?" Other Sociologist, October 14, 2011, accessed on July 20, 2015, http://othersociologist.com/otherness-resources/.

7　Anton Blok, *Honour and Violence* (Cambridge, UK: Polity, 2001); Yiannis Gabriel, "The Other and Othering—A Short Introduction" (blog), September 10, 2012, accessed on July 20, 2015, http://www.yiannisgabriel.com/2012/09/the-other-and-othering-short.html,.

8　M. M. Slaughter, "The Multicultural Self," *Cardozo Law Review* 14, no. 881 (1993): 885–91.

"othered."[9] Thus their racial identity is built in opposition to or in the denigration of others.[10]

Immigrants who phenotypically appear Black (as well as some non-White immigrants) often speak about their surprise upon arriving in the United States only to find that a denigrated "Black" identity is imposed on them. Othering springs from fear and the need to maintain an ego or a self whose esteem is based on maintaining an in-group membership. This kind of false self cannot be anything but insecure and unstable because it is dependent upon creating a certain definition of others to determine its meaning. Acknowledging this process helps to address the illusion that Blacks but not Whites are damaged by racism. Wendell Berry writes poignantly about this form of denial.

> If the white man has inflicted the wound of racism upon black men, the cost has been that he would receive the mirror image of that wound into himself. As the master, or as a member of the dominant race, he has felt little compulsion to acknowledge it or speak of it; the more painful it has grown the more deeply he has hidden it within himself. But the wound is there, and it is a profound disorder, as great a damage in his mind as it is in his society.[11]

Later in my teaching career, I developed courses on the self-concept, and race and ethnic identity. All kinds of students flocked to these courses in search of some understanding of their own constructed self-concepts and ambiguities about racial identity. I introduced research on self-esteem, gender, and racial identity. More importantly, I began to examine with my students where their ideas about self and race originated. Many students had never asked or answered questions like "Who am I?," "What are my primary identities?," and "What does it mean to be White or Black and where did I learn that?" During discussions of Whiteness, classes full of predominantly White students fell silent and I could feel the discomfort in the air. White students unable to discuss what it means to be White struggled primarily because of the history of the construction of the meaning of Whiteness.

---

9 Toni Morrison, *Playing in the Dark: Whiteness in the Literary Imagination* (New York: Vintage Books, 1993); Zevalios, "What Is Otherness?"

10 Irving, *Waking Up White*, 91.

11 Berry, *Hidden Wound*, 4.

Development of Whiteness in the United States

The United States has always grappled with race. From the time the English and other Europeans decided they had "discovered" and colonized a land already inhabited by "non-White" Native American and Mexican people, the mindset of White (mostly English and French) superiority prevailed. Initially, Irish, Italian, Polish, Jewish, and Greek immigrants were viewed as non-White.[12] The Great Migration of Blacks fleeing legalized vilification and violence in the Jim Crow south helped to alter this clearly socially constructed and malleable notion of Whiteness. Even today, although "Hispanic" is not a race, it is certainly a category of people that are considered non-White. Some biracial or multiracial individuals phenotypically look White, but are they really? Can phenotypically Black and White children come from the same parents and be siblings?[13]

Several writers describe how Whiteness is an unacknowledged social norm often equated with being American, dominant, and privileged.[14] Echoing Slaughter's work, Richard Dyer writes, "Other people are raced, we are just people."[15] We see evidence of this norm in news reporting, speeches, and writing about White people. Race is named to describe someone only if they are not White (Black minister, Chinese author, Indian doctor). Media tends to name race when a perpetrator is non-White but a White male suspect is typically referred to as a male suspect. Many Whites don't have to think about race and frequently remain unaware that they even possess one.[16] Toni Morrison writes cogently about this issue:

> Deep within the word "American" is its association with race. . . . American means white, and Africanist people struggle to make the term applicable to themselves with ethnicity and hyphen after hyphen after hyphen.[17]

---

12 James Barrett and David Roediger, "How White People Became White," in *White Privilege: Essential Readings on the Other Side of Racism*, ed. Paula Rothenberg (New York: Worth Publishers, 2011), 40–41.

13 Danzy Senna, *Caucasia* (New York: Riverhead Books, 1999).

14 Irving, *Waking Up White*; Morrison, *Playing in the Dark*.

15 Richard Dyer, "The Matter of Whiteness," in Rothenberg, *White Privilege*, 10.

16 Irving, *Waking Up White*, 91.

17 Morrison, *Playing in the Dark*, 47.

Developing a Positive Black Racial Identity: A Constant Struggle

After teaching race and ethnic identity courses for several years, I also came to see the damaging effects of racism on Black students. Clearly, there is much brokenness to repair from centuries of racial indignities. Among Blacks the wounds range from young Black children with dark skin who believe they are ugly or bad to Blacks physically attacking (i.e., assaulting or murdering) each other. The manifestation of the internalized social norms established during slavery whereby lighter skinned slaves were favored over darker skinned ones shows up in how some Blacks may berate each other based on their skin tones. Even today research studies indicate some differences in educational outcomes and sometimes economic disparities between light- and dark-skinned Blacks.[18] Evidence of a positive bias favoring lighter skinned Blacks by Whites and Blacks is present in the media, especially music videos, etc.

Perhaps less egregious but equally onerous are Blacks who narrowly define what it means to "act Black" and attack other Blacks for "acting White" if their behavior does not fall into a restricted realm of Black behavior. These labeling practices begin early when children are teased if they prefer or enjoy activities that are "non-stereotypically Black." Young Black children who like to read, seriously pursue academic work, love math and science, enjoy certain arts such as classical music, opera, or speak standard English or even dress in certain ways may be labeled as "acting white."[19] These ideas about Blackness are fueled by socially constructed meanings of race discussed earlier and reinforced by media portrayals of stereotypical versions of Blackness. With such a web of brainwashing and confused constructed meanings, it is not surprising that most people do not realize that they have internalized self-deprecation. This psychological jumble of representations illustrate the sordid outcome of my working definition of racism. Communication is far more powerful than people believe.

Just as Whites must unlearn the false construction that White is superior, Blacks have to heal and unlearn the belief that being Black is

---

18 Joni Hersch, "Skin-Tone Effects among African Americans: Perceptions and Reality," *The American Economic Review* (2006): 251–55.

19 S. John Ogbu Fordham, "Black Students' School Success: Coping with the 'Burden of "Acting White,"'" *The Urban Review* 18, no. 3 (1986): 176–206; Vinay Harpalani, "What Does 'Acting White' Really Mean?: Racial Identity Formation and Academic Achievement among Black Youth," *Urban Education Journal* 1, no. 1 (2002): 1–5, http://www.urbanedjournal.org/archive/volume-1-issue-1-spring-2002/what-does-acting-white-really-mean-racial-identity-formation-an

equated to being inferior. Old hurts and wounds keep Blacks imprisoned to the notion that they are "not enough" and often displace this hurt on each other. Such attacks limit the ability of *individuals* who are *Black* to feel and be authentic, to express themselves, to reach their full potential. If their real selves are obfuscated by false notions communicated to them by Blacks, Whites, and all who subscribe to same stereotypical thinking, how do they break out of this cycle? Unfortunately few people have learned that *phenotype* represents just the tip of the iceberg of the vast world that exists within each person. When I think or comment on my existence as a Black woman, I often say, "I am a Black woman and so much more."

Dismantling Racism One Interaction at a Time

As I moved toward midlife, a time that triggers self-examination and self-reflection, I once again revisited my ideas about race. I understood that in order to survive and thrive teaching in predominantly White institutions, I needed to reexamine what I had internalized about my racial identity. A precocious and observant child, I always felt smart and I worked hard. Because I attended integrated schools and became quite familiar with a variety of White children and families from an early age, I never learned to equate Whiteness with superiority. Yet as I grew older, I found those who did and reacted to me as such annoying, disruptive, and tiring. I spent years being angry, but over time I started feeling sorry for racist people because I knew they were suffering too, stuck in a lie and perhaps exhausted as well from having to defend and maintain a false sense of superiority.[20] I also learned to cherish my culture and history by educating myself about the contributions of Blacks to building America.

For many years I believed and hoped that altering psychological processes like changing the master status, making people aware of their projections and how they "other" people, would solve the problem with racism. With a growing awareness of how racism operates, for example, Amy Irving suggests in *Waking Up White* to try to trick the habit of categorizing a person first, focusing on one's master status. Clearly, one can *choose* to concentrate on a person's race, ethnic group, gender, height, or personal appearance or be curious about the *individual* beyond the phenotype. Typically when I engage with a person rather than my stereotype of him or her, I discover we possess some common ground. I correct

20 Berry, *Hidden Wound*, 4.

misperceptions ("missed" perceptions as I term it) that I displace on people every day. But I also realize that because racism is so embedded in our cognitive processes (sustaining implicit racial biases), and forms an essential component of one's self-concept, making these intentional changes may not be enough. People *see* what they believe. How then does one begin to teach and make people aware of racism, let alone learn to let it go? Perhaps exploring one's spirituality provides another approach.

Cultivating a Strong Spiritual Identity

As I worked with the White students who struggled with some vague sense of a White identity and Black students who possessed wounded Black identities, I noticed neither held any conception of a spiritual self. When I introduced William James's notion of spiritual self, the idea was completely foreign to them.[21] Were they aware of a self whose foundation was not socially constructed or reinforced by family, friends, and the media, by society, but emerged from Spirit?

Further, I also became aware of my need to explore and develop my own spiritual identity rather than to waste time and energy trying to change racist White people. It became evident why my mere presence as a competent, professional Black woman appeared threatening both to their self-concepts and perceptions of reality. I finally understood the anger and hostility of *people who think of themselves as White*. When they encountered me, they suffered a deep cognitive dissonance as well as fear. I needed to be attacked, eliminated, or dismissed. The very foundation of what it means to be White was called into question because it had been built upon a false definition of what it means to be Black.

Both personal medical crises and professional malaise motivated me to examine my spirituality more deeply. Having a strong spiritual identity anchored in God became the most powerful and essential tool to stepping around racism and racial discrimination. When denied an educational or occupational opportunity, often I received guidance through quiet listening about another often better position. Prayer that involved both asking and listening helped me to shift my dependence on the perceived powerful and dominant (e.g., White people, department chairs, deans) to the more powerful Spirit of God. Consequently, I walked away from overt and covert discrimination feeling like a victor rather than a victim.

---

21 William James, "The Self," reprinted in Chad Gordon, *The Self in Social Interaction,* vol. 1, ed. Kenneth Gergen (New York: John Wiley and Sons, 1968).

My Catholic background shaped my religious identity, which was mostly filled with fear about sin, guilt, confession, communion, and Jesus dying on the cross. In contrast, my budding spiritual identity began as a little girl who delighted in sitting in the wind. I loved being outside in nature, where I felt peaceful and a sense of wholeness. I couldn't name my experiences then. I didn't possess the vocabulary nor the cognitive ability to understand what a "peak" or mystical experience, a sense of unity meant. Yet my slowly emerging spiritual identity that stemmed from my active pursuit of and work on my personal relationship with God lay dormant for a number of years. Once unearthed through my introduction to readings about spirituality and meditation during college, and later by attending silent retreats, engaging in daily contemplative (listening) prayer, and pursuing spiritual direction training, my spiritual identity anchored me and buffered the blows from the needless ignorance and denial undergirding racism. I obtained encouragement through the life and writings of Howard Thurman, from his contemplative life that helped him cope with the horrors of growing up as a young Black boy and later a Black man in the early 1900s.[22]

Even though I continue to encounter racial stereotyping and bigotry from all kinds of people—Whites, Asians, Latinos, and even Blacks—I am aware that the fear and ignorance of others is something I need not internalize. An awareness that I believe emerges from engaging in a regular spiritual practice is key though to this unlearning process. Especially in times of crisis, an inner Voice, sometimes soft but on occasion much louder, guides and leads me.

Where Does Racial Harmony Exist?

One way to heal the racial divide is to observe under what conditions racial harmony exists or flourishes. I notice most progress with racism occurs in situations and organizations where people have to work together for their common survival, their common good. Thus, during natural disasters and collective life-threatening crises, people seem to be able to put racial issues aside to help and care for one another.

I also notice a dampening of racial agitation in some spiritual domains. I do not necessarily mean churches or church groups, but more so in those places and spaces where the emphasis is on spirit, the primary focus is on awakening and feeding the spirit. There is a qualitatively different

---

22 Thurman, *With Head and Heart.*

experience in interacting with people who have developed strong spiritual identities and who are more identified with them than their other social identities like race, gender, or occupational status. Racial tensions frequently recede into the background at retreat centers, for example, where the focus is on God, prayer, stillness, and silence.

Retreat centers are ideal because they are prayer-filled spaces and the purpose for being there is to nurture one's relationship with God. Typically hosted by nuns, monks, or people dedicated to God and prayer, my sense is that they see and embrace me as a fellow spirit or spiritual pilgrim seeking God as well. Typically a deep peace prevails. However, this is not to say that on occasion I encounter pilgrims who are in the early stages of cultivating their spiritual identities and thus respond to me based on their stereotypes of Black women instead of as a fellow spiritual pilgrim. Yet because I am there to nurture my spirit, it is easier for me to smile, bless them, and return to my silent retreat.

Likewise in contemplative/listening prayer/meditation groups and in spiritual direction, racial differences aren't ignored, but they typically do not control or dominate the conversations. My integrated spiritual director peer group serves as a prime example. We operate and refer to each other as Spirit Sisters and meet regularly in a supportive environment that allows for self-disclosure. Frequently, these groups are interfaith or interdenominational and members are intentional in gathering together to support each other's *spiritual* lives. And we learn about the commonalities we share with people who are members of different racial and ethnic groups. Our egos (constructed selves) compete for wealth, status, and power, but spirits collaborate to awaken each other to our spiritual self. Thus, racism appears to evaporate anywhere the ego does not prevail.

Conclusion—The Journey toward Wholeness

I often wonder what happened to Karen Gallo and if we would encounter the same racial dynamics if we would enter first grade together now. I suspect that our early Catholic education, which oriented us toward God, assisted us in deconstructing the respective racial identities imposed on us and later building strong spiritual identities. Little did we know then what a strong impact these early experiences would have on our life journeys.

Thus, I believe racism is a mental "dis-EASE" whose primary albeit often unconscious drive is to attack what is different, what might appear frightening. It feeds a fear that separates rather than fuels a love that joins and connects us as holy children of God. Racism manifests in other cultures as "ethnic cleansing," xenophobia, or anti-immigrant sentiment. For the racism in the United States is just a microcosm, a representation of group conflicts all over the world. Yet when will we master this essential spiritual lesson? Hopefully it will be learned before countless more generations suffer unnecessary and senseless violence and dehumanization.

The unlearning of racist tendencies involve some serious self-examination and self-reflection. To move beyond the blame game, it is vital that each of us ponder our own identities, where they originated and how they motivate us now. Answering simple but provocative questions like, "Who am I?," "Who taught me who I am?," or "How does my racial identity direct my thinking, my feelings, my behavior about myself and toward others?" provide a springboard. Similar questions may stimulate an inner scrutiny and offer some insights into the underpinnings of how each and every one of us is socialized to be racist. It is in these moments of introspection that we can unpack the perceptual biases that reinforce separation and deny our interconnection. Perusing the meditations offered by Howard Thurman, for example, is an excellent way to initiate this process.[23]

Sociologists posit that the meaning of our social identities like race is negotiated in the midst of social interactions. Each of us is an active agent in that negotiation and we must respond accordingly. Socially constructed selves are filled with variety of identities that can create a psychological prison. Just as Alice Miller assisted depressed people in letting go of false selves,[24] we can also facilitate healthy mental health by letting go of the false selves that are related to race. Therefore, restructuring or reconfiguring one's racial identity and self-concept are possible, albeit often painful.[25]

Again awareness is key to unlearning the cognitive biases associated with racism. As adults, that process begins with becoming compassionate observers of our own behavior and taking note to correct our transgressions. How do we automatically respond to young Black males, women wearing the hijab or burka? How do we "other" people even within our own families or faith communities?

---

23 Howard Thurman, *Meditations of the Heart* (Boston: Beacon Press Friends United Press, 1981); Howard Thurman, *The Centering Moment* (Richmond, IN: Friends United Press, 1969).

24 Alice Miller, *The Drama of the Gifted Child: The Search for the True Self*, rev. ed. (New York: Basic Books, 1996).

25 Irving, *Waking Up White*.

The dismantling of racism begins as each of us becomes increasingly aware of our spiritual self, a self anchored in a more consistent, true, and stable being in God. A regular spiritual practice: personal quiet time (e.g., "listening" prayer), reading of spiritual material (e.g., Roberta Bondi, Thomas Kelly, Richard Rohr, Howard Thurman), journaling, classes in spiritual formation, viewing the vast amount of programs about spirituality available online or on television, contemplative prayer groups, silent retreats or quiet days—all facilitate spiritual growth.[26]

For some people this work is accomplished easier in groups, maybe in Sunday school, on retreats, or during a Wednesday night gathering. Silence is always helpful. A posing of questions followed by a few minutes of silence or the stilling of one's thoughts allows more fruitful solutions to bubble up in a quiet rather than chattering mind.

In conclusion, there is something "normal" about diversity. It exists in nature, in wildlife, and the ecosystem cannot sustain itself without a variety of interdependent species. Likewise we as human beings need what each individual offers in our vast world of diverse people, religions, and ways of perceiving the world. We cannot survive without each other. We cannot flourish unless we find ways to look beyond physical appearances to see the magnificent spirits God created. We must connect with "others," with people who look different from ourselves for completion, for healthy wholeness, for true holiness. Wendell Berry captures this sentiment brilliantly.

> It may be the most significant irony in our history that racism, by dividing the two races, has made them not separate but in a fundamental way inseparable, not independent but dependent on each other, incomplete without each other, each needing desperately to understand and make use of the experience of the other. After so much time together we are one body, and the division between us is the disease of one body, not two. Even the white man and the black man who hate each other are, by that very token, each other's emotional dependents.[27]

---

26 Roberta Bondi, *Memories of God* (New York: Abingdon Press, 1995); T. Kelly, *A Testament to Devotion* (New York: Harper-One, 1981); R. Rohr, *Everything Belongs: The Gift of Contemplative Prayer*, rev. and updated (New York: Crossroad Books, 2003); Thurman, *Meditations of the Heart* and *Centering Prayer*.

27 Berry, *Hidden Wound*, 78.

3 Why Is This Black Woman Still Talking about Race?

Catherine Meeks

Even before I learned about race, I knew that I was different. I was not sure what the difference was until my parents told me the reasons why I could not go to the front window at the Dairy Queen, try on the new dress that I wanted, or sit in the same waiting room with White people in our little rural Arkansas town. And even learning about the reasons for these things still did little to communicate the real issues to me.

My father was an illiterate sharecropper and my mother was a teacher who graduated from college the same year that I graduated from high school. Mama had attended evening and Saturday classes and taken correspondence courses to finally graduate. She had been in school during my entire childhood. She had begun teaching in the era when grades 1–8 were in the same room and the teacher was not required to have a college degree.

Watching my parents labor under the burden of the inequality that having black skin brought to our lives made a deep and lasting impression upon me. Along with this was another deep and unforgettable lesson. A lesson learned from the story that my father told more often than I wish he had. It was the story of my brother Garland's death. A death from which my father never recovered.

My brother began complaining of stomach pain that did not respond to all the home remedies that were tried. Finally, the pain was unbearable and my father got someone to drive the two of them to the hospital in El Dorado, about twenty-five miles from where we lived. Because we were poor and Black, the hospital refused to treat my brother and instructed my father to take him to the "charity" hospital in Shreveport, Louisiana, about seventy miles from our house. By the time my father could get someone to drive them there, Garland's appendix had become so infected that he was beyond saving when they finally reached the hospital. He died soon after arriving. He was twelve years old.

I heard this story on a regular basis from my father because he grieved about Garland until he died. He was angry about his lack of ability to save his son. His poverty and his skin color were two major strikes against him. He could not do anything about either one of them. The sense of being immobilized often made my father mean to us. As an adult, I understand that dynamic now, but as a child it was confusing and frightening to me. I loved my father and I wanted to be pleasing and acceptable to him and that was very hard to do because he was so dissatisfied with himself and his plight in life. My father's plight made it clear to me that I wanted to seek another path; a path to power that would not leave me feeling helpless and hopeless. Though at the time I had no idea that these early experiences would shape the deep and undying commitment I now have about working for racial healing, I knew that I had to do something. My early life was not connected to White people beyond the point of seeing them as having what we needed and keeping us from it. Since my father was a sharecropper, we lived on the land of a White man, we shopped in his store, and we were basically at his mercy. My father was always sad and disappointed about the outcome of the year-end settlement after the harvest of the crops. He was never able to get ahead financially in spite of all of the hard work that we had done for the year. This cycle of glorified slavery which is commonly called sharecropping was another factor in removing the last prospect of hope from my father.

So at a very deep level, I made a decision that my life had to be different. First of all, I had to seek something larger than the world in which I lived my daily life. I began that search by reading everything that I could get my hands on and listening to the radio to hear what I could about a world that did not seem to be a part of anything I knew. Along with this came my thirst for education. It seemed to me that education would help me to create a better life than the one I watched my father live.

It also seemed clear to me that something more than education was required in order to live in this world where people who looked like my family and me seemed to be singled out for suffering. I was not sure what to make of this and I wondered what God had to do with it. My questions were forming at a very early age about race, faith, and the ultimate quest to be a human being.

There were no people with whom to talk about any of this when I was younger; my family did not talk much about race except to point out the pain associated with being Black and staying in the place that would be the safest for us. My father and mother were fearful about our safety and some of their behavior seemed designed only to control us. In fact, it was their effort to protect us. They had lost one child to racism and they did not intend to lose another one. I understand that fear now, though it was not understandable to me as young girl who wanted to be free.

My search for the answer to what it means to be a human being who happens to inhabit a black body propelled me through many years. The question has complex and complicated answers involving being willing to look deep within my own soul while seeing the world through lenses that contributed to my discomfort. A discomfort that arose from my preconceived notions and what I found actually to be true.

Thoughts on the Myth of Race

Some of the literature I have studied and taught reflects on race as a myth constructed to help in categorizing people as well as making the construction of oppressive systems possible. I understand the truth of this notion of race as a construction and believe that all people are connected. What happens to one of us happens to all of us in the deepest sense.

However, the idea of race as myth or construction is not easy to swallow in the light of racism. Oppressive systems and hierarchical structures that make it possible for twelve-year-old Black boys to die from lack of medical care and old men to live a lifetime of helplessness and hopelessness cause too much pain to simply erase by dismissing race as a construct.

Even though there is not much conversation about this notion outside of academic settings, it is one that needs to occur far more broadly. The conversation might be easier to facilitate if race had been allowed to stand alone as a prejudicial factor instead of being coupled with notions of inferiority and superiority. These additions layered onto the construct of race complicated the matter of attempting to establish a way to differentiate physical characteristics. Race as an illusion sounds wonderful in theory but race seems never to be divorced from the notion of superiority and inferiority. Therefore, it is not reasonable to simply attempt to erase racism by asserting that race is an illusion. It is not an illusion to the souls inhabiting bodies of color.

As a child, I was determined to feel better someday about living in the body that had been assigned to me. I knew that I had to learn to live in the world with White people and my faith taught me that these same folks who created the pain and suffering that my family experienced were connected to me in some way. For a large part of my early life I simply lived as if the connection was not true, but during my college years I had to grapple with the dissonance caused by my intellectual understanding of the connection and my heart's rejection of it. As I moved through those years, many opportunities to see what I had never seen before began to emerge for me.

Pepperdine College Days

During my days at the small liberal arts church-related Pepperdine College, I had the opportunity to embrace the head and heart struggle that had come to be my constant companion in more ways than I could have ever believed possible. First of all, I became involved in a house church that was predominantly White and on campus I was a part of the Black Students Association. This was in the late sixties, the era of internal and external conflict about racial identity and the political issues surrounding the struggle for racial liberation.

While the house church helped me to strengthen my faith perspective, it did not help me with the identity issues. The folks who participated in the house church, while not unconscious about race, did not grasp the depths of the issue for the few Blacks who came to the gathering. The idea of colorblindness did not allow for addressing race in a fulsome or helpful way. "Colorblindness" is a basic denial of the reality of race, which can undermine serious conversation. It was difficult for me to make sense of the relationships that I was developing with my White peers while I lived in the world of Black struggle.

There were four mentors brought into my life who continue to be an integral part of my journey. They were the dean of women, the dean of students and his wife, and the head resident in the dormitory. These four people, all of whom were White, were able to see me as the person that I really was as well as the person that I could become. They were able to be accepting. Their acceptance became a part of the foundation that I built during those years which has continued to provide me a source of courage and hope as I continue to travel along the path of racial healing.

These folks were able to demonstrate the difference between trying to be colorblind and not creating a racial barrier too large to cross in order to be loving and accepting. They were the first White people I had ever known who were able or interested in doing this. They worked for the good of all students and they did not have any notions about Black exceptionalism. All of us Black students were seen as the valuable human beings that we were. In that era of campus unrest, they fought for us even when it caused them to suffer.

Though it would be many years before I developed a strong unwavering voice in regards to racial healing, those college years contributed mightily. It was during that time that I began to realize that neither White colorblindness nor Black rage can successfully participate in the process of building a community of equity where acceptance is possible. The foundational work of these years made it possible for me to embrace the teachings of C. G. Jung and Howard Thurman later in my life as I continued to look for the ways to incorporate my Black female body with my humanity and to understand what that incorporation had to do with living with others on the planet.

Encountering the "Other" on the Inner Journey

According to C. G. Jung, projection is an important part of the relationship dynamic. It is the shadow which undergirds the process of projection because it contains the parts of the human personality that is generally hidden or unknown and is seeking to be revealed.[1] Projection occurs when these hidden qualities are assigned to persons in our community and labeled as "other"; taken a step further, they become the primary tools in creating oppressive structures.

Individuals, groups, and nations can engage in a similar process of assigning unknown, disliked, or hidden areas of the personality to others. This process relieves one from having to take responsibility for shortcomings or unwanted behaviors. It also helps to remove the need to accept one's role in the misfortunes that might come into one's life as a result of bad choices by assigning responsibility for negative outcomes to others. The best example of this at the personal level can be seen in the addict who cannot accept responsibility for substance abuse, persisting in blaming external circumstances for their addiction.

This psychological dynamic is complex but universal. No one is

---

1   Edward C. Whitmont, *The Symbolic Quest* (Princeton, NJ: Princeton University Press, 1969), 160–62.

exempt. Therefore everyone needs to pay attention and do the work necessary to become awake to hidden inner qualities so that their external
behaviors can be aligned with their inner desires. This leads one to a life
of authenticity.

I met Dr. Howard Washington Thurman, who spoke eloquently about
the human imperative to align one's head and heart, first through his
writings, then in person, and later in the fine British Broadcasting Film
interviews with him about his journey from a little boy in Florida to the
halls of academia and the founding of the Church for the Fellowship of
All Peoples. He brought such good news to my journey through his wise
teaching and the way he embodied the challenge of being a human being
who happened to be contained in a Black body. His clear assertion that
one has to explore one's inner depths to learn what is contained at the
core resonated with the understanding I was gleaning from my work
with Jungian thinking about the shadow.

The hidden qualities in each person want to be revealed and when
one understands this deepest inner makeup, the externals become less
important. Oppression cannot gain a stronghold in such a person because
their understanding of reality is rooted at a level beyond the reach of the
external world. When this happens, one is able to accept whatever comes
without being derailed. It is this type of personal inner work that creates
the empowered life which can be lived beyond the reach of racial identity.
It is not that skin color goes away; it becomes unimportant because the
definition of one's self occurs at a deeper level with a clear understanding
that the meaning of personhood goes beyond race, gender, sexual orientation, behavior, or possessions. This journey into the depths of the self is
true for every human being, but for those who are oppressed, it is a vital
journey if there is ever to be any true liberation.

Since everyone has a Jungian shadow side, the process of becoming
whole demands the critical work of encountering and appropriating
what is found there in ways far beyond simply reassigning those qualities to unsuspecting others. Howard Thurman, more than anyone that I
know of, lived this truth out in his daily life. The desire to be free can be
a catalyst for this part of the journey as it has been for many who have
never heard of Jung or Thurman.

Often, when I contrast my father's grief, which had no place to go,
with Thurman's understanding that all of life is managed by that inner
barometer, I am sorry that my father was not able to make such a connection in his own way. However, I am never without gratitude in finding
this path myself and I continue to pray that my father might benefit in

some manner by the fact that his child is not suffering as he did. I hope that the healing goes back and forth.

It is this process of self-integration that makes it possible for individuals to build bridges across fears and differences, finding ways to trust one another and have true relationships. Blacks cannot hedge their bets when connecting with Whites and play a game of make-believe trust which does not allow for genuine relationship to develop. And Whites cannot play the exceptionalism game and see their Black friend as an exception to other Blacks. There has to be a willingness to accept the person and to hold the cultural constructs that debilitate all of us at the same time. Yes, it creates a disturbance in one's head to do this, but it is a necessary disturbance if the true bridge-building required for authentic racial healing is to take place.

However, it is clear that being vulnerable to one another will not occur unless those who are engaging in the relationship-building process have done the inner work which will allow them a place of inner security that can sustain the process. The confrontation with one's individual hidden qualities (shadow) and owning those qualities without the temptation of assigning them to another person through projection is as necessary in building relationships across racial lines as in any other relationship-building efforts.

It seems that much of the race relationship-building work of the past, especially in religious communities, has been done on the basis of Whites attempting to become colorblind and finding a handful of Blacks who can be seen as exceptions and Blacks finding a few Whites who can be tolerated because they make certain kinds of helpful contributions to them and other Black people. Otherwise, we would not find ourselves at this point in the twenty-first century: standing on the edge of racial disaster as violence increases and disillusionment grows with the effort to create a Beloved Community (a place where oneness is affirmed).

Later on in this chapter we will discuss some of the work that will be required in the building of Beloved Community, but it is important not to leave the discussion about the necessity of the inner work too quickly. There is no substitute for it. There are no short cuts and no one is exempt.

Perhaps one of the most important questions to ask today is: Can White, Black, and Brown people form authentic relationships built on trust, love, and acceptance? It is not a simple question, but it is one that we have to answer. The fate of the earth depends upon us finding a way to do this. The earth cannot contain the continued racial strife that informs all aspects of our life together. If we can learn to withdraw our shadow enough to see the face of God in each other, we can build those relationships and we can change the way our world is traveling.

While this challenge for me has been centered around Whites and Blacks, it involves everyone. As a Southerner, I have the legacy of my region as well as the more global issues of race to confront. But the good news is that the shadow work can be universalized into all arenas. When those hidden qualities are confronted, the positive energy from that work extends throughout and just as the whole person will benefit, so the whole community will benefit from each person doing his or her inner work. Following the individual inner path to wholeness can benefit the community.

In the long run the community will be strengthened by the personal power and energy generated by the persons who are living with better integration between their hearts and heads and with less reason to project anything either negative or positive onto anyone else. They will be more confident in claiming their own weakness and their own power and will find it completely unnecessary to assign anything to another person. In this type of environment there is a great opportunity for the Beloved Community to develop, a place where people see the face of God in one another and know that each time they encounter another person, God is present.

The Outer Journey

In early 1975 I moved from Los Angeles to Macon, Georgia. It was a difficult transition for me to make but taught me a great deal about the outer journey, and the following story will help to frame the comments that I want to make about that side of the journey.

I hunted for a church when I first moved to Macon, so when I was invited to attend Northside Christian Church, I was delighted. I drove across town to the church one Sunday morning filled with great hope that it might be a place I could make my church home. When I walked in, the congregation was singing, so I was waiting until the song was finished before entering. I was greeted by an usher, who looked nervous, and walked away. Though I had not paid much attention to him, it was soon clear that he had gone to inform the male leaders of the church that I was there. While I was waiting, a group of ten men approached me and the leader of them asked, "What is your business here this morning?" Needless to say, I was stunned. I said my name and that "I came there to worship because some friends had invited me." He said, "You don't have any friends here." Then I told them their names and he looked at me as if I were making the story up. So I said, "What's the matter? Don't you let Black people come to this church?" He responded, "No, we don't."

So, since I was not there to do anything but worship, I turned and walked out of the building, got in my car, rolled up my windows, and locked the door. Then I burst into tears. I had never been thrown out of a church before. After a few minutes I got myself together and drove off. As I was driving down the road, a beautiful deer ran out of the woods, requiring that I stop for it—then a second one followed it, and then a third one—and all of them ran across the road in front of my car. I waited in amazement.

"Father, Son, and Holy Spirit" were the words that came into my mind immediately. That realization was followed by the thought that God wanted to assure me that the behavior of those folks inside that structure that had named itself a church was not the end of the story. The behavior I had experienced a few moments before was not the whole story, but only a piece of it and I needed to be reminded of that in an unforgettable manner. Prior to that morning, three deer had never paraded in front me as those did and it has never happened again.

I am convinced that the work of dismantling racism and oppression cannot be done without great injury to the soul unless the worker has the capacity to pay attention to the ways in which the effort is supported both by the external community and the spirit within. I was hurt by my experience that Sunday morning but comforted by the deer who spoke for God to me. A few days later, the pastor of that church called me. He had gotten my phone number from my friends who were very angry by the way I had been treated. He told me that they "never had a problem with race before." I responded, "You have always had a problem; you just did not know it. So you should be thankful that I showed up because this is an issue that as pastor you need to address." He agreed and asked if he could come to visit me. I said that he could but felt that his congregation needed visiting more than I did.

Actually I had recovered a bit from the affront and I was not anxious to speak to him, but he did eventually come. I was not especially impressed by his visit. He told me that many of the members were very upset about what had happened and that his congregation was in an uproar. Of course that was fine with me; they needed to be in an uproar. The church has no business ever turning anyone away.

The resilience that one needs to engage such assaults comes from engaging in the inner work that has been discussed. But the outer work has to be done with the same degree of determination as the inner work is embraced. The structures of oppression have to be torn down. Institutions that were constructed around the idea of the superiority of one group over another because of skin color have no right to continue to exist as they are. It takes more than mere cosmetic changes to create a culture of equality for every person, regardless of skin color.

Many things are different today because scores of brave and freedom-hungry people took stands against all odds to make changes and they did. Those of us who are the twenty-first-century beneficiaries of their courage and sacrifices cannot lay the banner down, claiming weariness or any other reason for not continuing to march on down the road.

Clearly we have not finished the race. Our nation has tried to live in the illusory world of having become a "postracial" culture, but events of the past years bear witness to how far we are from being "postracial." Perhaps the election of President Barack Obama did more to make this point crystal clear than any other single act of the past ten years. The shock of having a Black person hold the highest office in the land, the office that was supposed to be held by White men only was more than those White men continuing to hold notions of White male supremacy could tolerate. While the civil rights gains of the past were not pleasing to the White male supremacist, they were not as devastating to his sense of identity as losing the White House to a Black man.

Thus all of the efforts to maintain equilibrium are disturbed. The politics have become more fractured than ever. White men are in general disarray. White male violence is reasserting itself in unsettling ways as is seen in the police killings of young Black people, especially males. The sense of powerlessness is manifestly evident in the Tea Party cry, "We want our country back." That cry is not lost on anyone who is listening. The projection of superiority has been dealt a serious blow and rightly so. There can be no major change until the shadow is owned. When the White supremacist honestly acknowledges that their projection of superiority is not true, the real process of building something new can begin.

The work of protests will continue to help in creating an environment where the shadow-projected illusions cannot be contained. The main structures that support those illusions have to be dismantled. This critical process can be seen around the country as old symbols are being challenged. Symbols such as the Confederate flag and the names of buildings and monuments that were constructed in honor of people who were racists are being changed. Though there are some who would attempt to revise history so we can forget our past, this process is not being supported as they would hope. History cannot be erased simply by replacing it with lies.

This work has to be done. There are no shortcuts and no one is exempt. The ways that we do the external work depends in large part upon who we are. While everyone should be concerned about the common good and all of us need to do whatever we can to dismantle oppressive structures, we will not all be doing the same thing at the same time, but all of us should be on the freedom-seeking journey all of the time.

Standing up for justice and dismantling oppressive structures requires the development of new ways of seeing and aligning the external and internal work so that our lives are not destroyed by unbalanced activism. We can do better than this by paying attention to our own needs and those of others and developing our work around models of compassion.

Dismantling structures of oppression is critical and it is the work of warrior women and men that will get it done. Warriors, however, need to be cared for lest they lose themselves and end up angry and bitter with no sense of hope to share. The need for health and balance must stay at the forefront of all that is done in the struggle for change.

Repentance and Reconciliation

There will be no racial reconciliation in America without justice. There will be no justice without racial healing. Whites who wish to do the work of dismantling racism have to realize this truth. Over the years there has been much talk about racial reconciliation and many people who are thinking seriously about this work have grown very weary of the conversation. The weariness comes because the notion of reconciliation without justice is much akin to the idea of cheap grace. Racial healing is the foundation upon which justice and reconciliation will be built.

This rush to racial reconciliation is rooted deeply in the notion of colorblindness. This philosophy is highly held in the religious communities of America; it is not, however, a notion that is rooted in truly trying to hear what Blacks are saying about their state of affairs when it comes to race. It becomes an effort to edit the commentary of the Black experience and to name it in ways that do not demand real systemic change.

The more concrete examples of this can be found in the yearly pulpit swaps in which some churches engage, bringing a Black and White congregation together once or twice a year to have a meal or some type of program—the enthusiastic celebration of Martin Luther King Day activities or the celebration of Black history month programs—without plans for continuing the work and without any intention to honestly seek ways to make life better for Blacks and other people of color.

Some readers will recall the notion of cheap grace being grace that allows one to enjoy its benefits without requiring accountability for the ways in which one chooses to live daily life. The connection is clear: symbolic gestures and occasional gatherings without a commitment to relationship and Beloved Community is cheap. If the voices who wish to speak are to be considered viable, a new perspective is necessary: one that embraces the concept of justice and the need for racial healing.

The understanding of repentance as the willingness to "change one's mind" speaks to the point that I am making here. Whites who become conscious and accept the systemic constructions that grant them privileges because of the color of their skin will need to change their minds in order to see those structures dismantled.

While this is true for Whites, there is repentance work for Blacks as well. We have to "change our minds" about the internalized oppression that we have allowed ourselves to succumb to and the ways in which that negative energy has been given an opportunity to thrive. Of course, there are no structures that have been constructed to advantage Blacks while disadvantaging Whites. Even in the instances when Blacks have some degree of delegated power to practice prejudice, they still cannot claim ownership of the systems of power that prevail in America as Whites can do. But the internalization of the oppression that has been projected onto Blacks and the willingness to replicate those ideas in the ways that Blacks relate to other Blacks cannot continue if true racial healing is to be realized and if justice is to find its way into the fabric of our culture in ways that make our society one where equity is practiced and the Beloved Community can be realized. A discussion of particular strategies that can help move this process along for Blacks will be presented in the next chapter.

Repentance for Whites, that is, the willingness to change one's mind, looks quite a bit different than it does for Blacks and it is necessary if true racial healing is to come to our land. While many Whites feel strongly that having had nothing to do with construction of the current systems they are exempt from any accountability regarding them, part of the healing process requires a close examination of the benefits enjoyed by White persons from those systems and the embracing of those benefits. There is a primary question to be answered. Does the White person enjoy the benefits of the current systems of power and accept them as a part of their normal life or does the person realize that Blacks and other people of color do not enjoy those same benefits? Once that realization is made, what does the individual do? When hearing a Black person's account of exclusion from such benefits, is there an effort to resist the temptation to explain away the other's experience? The willingness to listen and believe the Black person and to respect the rights to feelings and perceptions is a critical piece of "changing one's mind."

Along with this, Blacks must have the courage to ensure that their story is not edited. While this is a tiring enterprise, it is worth the effort because it helps to create the honest exchange that is essential if change is to occur.

To change one's mind is never a simple process and it is especially challenging when that change means that certain lifestyle changes are required as well. It is difficult for Whites to see themselves as White and to see the systemic constructions of power as oppressive because their skin and the structures have been named as normal. Therefore, it takes an enormous amount of intentionality to allow the necessary change of mind. It is easier to explain the situation in other ways than to see how the systems have been constructed. Relinquishing power is never easy.

When Blacks have more power, what will be done with it? It is critical not simply to follow the model demonstrated by Whites. It is much the same dilemma that women face in terms of having power while not behaving as men have behaved. Though Blacks have seen oppression dynamics modeled very effectively, it is a model that they can ill afford to replicate. Therefore, the "change of mind" or repentance requires the deep inner and external work that will create new models. Of course there will be trial and error in this process and some efforts will be more successful than others, but a complete paradigm shift is necessary for the healing process to run its full course. Black people will have to withdraw whatever negative projections from other Blacks they might have and work to see the face of God in one another in a way that creates new spaces for life to emerge. The temptation to continue the master narrative cannot be obliged.

Perhaps the reader is skeptical about whether or not such a great shift can occur and wonders what it might look like if and when it does happen. While it is impossible to know exactly what it will be, it is not too difficult to imagine. The imaginative process involves being willing to take into consideration a world that truly practiced the notion of the worth and equality of each individual: a world where power is used for the common good and not to benefit any group and where a genuine intention exists to provide for basic needs to be met; a world in which no one was denied their fundamental human rights and with a commitment to the notion that all lives are connected, with no one expendable. This is a good description of the Beloved Community where life is reverenced and neither physical or psychological violence are viable options for getting the business of the day done.

This is far from being a utopia, as some might be tempted to lament. This is simply a world operating on the basic premises that the United States Constitution has already made a claim to support: the idea of supporting the common good and promoting the general welfare. Of course it is clear in terms of the course of history that these words did not mean what they appear to mean, but the good news is that centuries ago the carvers of the Constitution were imagining a better world than they had the will to create.

So if, in the remainder of the twenty-first century and in the centuries to come, all people could work to make this world a reality, what good work that would be. The operating systems for this Republic will have to be revisioned and reconstructed. Is it possible to do this work in peace, harmony, and with a sense of shared fellowship? That is the question that must always remain before us. Can we do this work in a peaceful and nonviolent manner?

We haven't done it, but does that mean we cannot or simply that we will not? We can change our minds and we can change our hearts. We can look to our history for examples of some of the ways oppressive systems have been deconstructed. Remember, however, that we have not done the work without protests and often violence serving as the catalyst and even when laws have been changed, those changes have been forced and the head—and heart—changes may not have occurred.

Voting rights are a great example. Most people who witnessed that historic change in the political structure would never have guessed that a few decades later, parts of that law would be struck down by the Supreme Court and that similar laws would be in jeopardy as detractors sought ways to avoid obeying them. While the laws have to change, those changes are insufficient unless the will of the people is reconstructed.

How does the will of the people become reconstructed? How is a consciousness developed that leads to Whites seeing themselves in terms of their privilege and to repentance? When this type of transformation occurs, it is not necessary to long for days that have come and gone. The present becomes acceptable. Reality—individually and collectively—can be reshaped as the direct result of this type of personal transformation.

This type of change can be painful. Unfortunately, efforts to escape the pain lead us to move quickly to reconciliation instead of staying with the notion of justice and racial healing. It is not easy for Blacks or Whites to embrace this deep transforming change because it means that everything will be different; there is great fear that personal loss will come with the change. History has borne out the dangers involved in the process, as some who have worked for such change actually lost their lives. This is not to be taken lightly. Though transformation around White privilege should not require physical death, it does require a psychological shift that can seem like a death experience. This shift often requires a redefinition of one's self and a new vantage point when interacting in the world. That is not always easy to determine; many people never find the courage to embark upon this journey to racial consciousness and healing and the transformation it can bring.

Thus the structures of oppression can be camouflaged as the source of security. When this is the case, it is very difficult to believe that one's life can be acceptable without them. Thus fear arises and when fear becomes the motivator for behavior, there is no way to predict where the process will lead and what many will be willing to do in order to preserve the status quo. Our country knows this dynamic very well and we have the scars of violence to prove it.

We can hope and pray while we work to make sustainable changes that fear will not become the response Whites choose to embody and that the need to create a more perfect union can rise above the fear. As Whites who become more conscious speak and act courageously enough to affect the country, repentance, "the changing of minds," and justice can emerge, making it possible for racial healing and reconciliation to follow and authentic healing to be realized.

Conversation Must Continue

I keep talking about race because dialogue has to continue. When we stop talking to one another, our negative projections and deepest fears create an illusory tale that makes it impossible to build any type of community. It is in talking to one another that we learn about each other. We can build bridges through the knowledge we gain from our conversations, helping us to move beyond simplistic first impressions based on skin color. It takes such foundations to sustain us during efforts to keep the status quo intact. As it is, we have allowed so many distractions to infiltrate our lives, genuine conversations are difficult. The challenge of social media and other types of technology that help us to distance ourselves cannot be ignored in this discussion. It is easy to opt for the superficial rather than the authentic as we engage one another in our current cultural milieu.

It is important to take a chance. The efforts we make each day to connect with one another may lead to a day when the system of oppression will be destroyed. Each authentic daily struggle can lead to a weakening of the overall system and one day it will collapse. Just as the water slowly running over the side of a mountain for hundreds of years can carve a path through the rock, so is the work of authentic conversation. It will carve away at the foundation of racist practice and be replaced by the foundation built from the slow, consistent, and persistent relationship building that occurs between Blacks and Whites who are faithful to the call. That is why I keep talking.

CHAPTER 4

Mama, It Is So Hard to Be Black in America

Catherine Meeks

ama, it is so hard to be Black in America," lamented my oldest son after the Charleston Nine Massacre. My son's lament has haunted me ever since. Two experiences during my son, Mbye's, school years vividly foreshadowed the challenges he would face as a Black man. With his Quiz Bowl team near Valdosta, Georgia, he was insulted by a local police officer. Walking with team members back to their hotel, the policeman drove up beside my son and asked, "Do you want some peanuts?" Mbye said, "No." "Well, you should, because you look like a monkey." Frightened by the comment, Mbye began running back to the hotel.

On another occasion, one of his teachers criticized Mbye and one of his classmates for their African names. She thought their names had been contrived in some manner instead of realizing that both children were native-born Africans. My son was born in Gambia and his friend in Nigeria.

In both cases, I demanded that the adults involved write letters of apology. In both cases, the children were surprised that an offending adult had been held accountable and that their insult and injury had not gone unnoticed. My insistence was to help the children involved realize that they are not powerless in the face of racism.

When small racist acts are allowed to go unchecked, they cluster in the psyche and damage one's self-esteem. While a single act may be distasteful but seem to deserve little attention, the collective power is deadly; the ongoing acceptance of small acts of racism and the negative projections that may incite them contributes to the process of internalized oppression. For centuries Black people have struggled with the projection of a false reality based upon the notion of White supremacy. Black skin, hair, and ways of living in the world have been presumed inferior as all things White were considered normative and desirable. While the study of history helps us to understand the foundation for this notion of superiority, it does not help one to overcome it more easily.

Being Black in America never leaves the consciousness. The charge of "playing a race card," ludicrous as the concept may be, is usually leveled at an individual describing an experience of racism, but the Black person is not trusted to tell his or her own story. The presumptive normative nature of White supremacy makes the editing of the Black person's assessment seem appropriate, a process designed, consciously or not, to place the blame on something other than racism.

It is popular these days to describe these acts and efforts as being microaggressions. In fact, they are not "micro" at all, though they are certainly aggressions. These are acts of denigration based upon race and cannot be allowed to go unremarked. These acts come from the norm of White supremacy and they are never harmless. The tricky part of these projections is that those upon whom the projections are made can easily accept them as true. When that happens, the recipients of the projections began to live in ways that make the projections seem to be a legitimate part of themselves. This is a significant means by which oppression becomes internalized. Internalized oppression may even manifest itself through the preoccupation that many Blacks have with skin color or hair quality and in the ways that members within the community are treated based upon these external qualities.

When negative projections become the bases for the social constructions that serve to oppress Blacks and other people of color, they begin to be lived out in ways that make them culturally acceptable. Consider the projection of the Black male as dangerous to the White woman. Black men continue to be seen as more dangerous than anyone else but in actuality it was White men who were most dangerous during slavery and Reconstruction because they were orchestrating the forces of oppression. This continues today with mass incarceration. Black men have internalized that negative message and their behavior can make them more vulnerable to a system that is designed to subdue and control them. It is easy to fall into living the expectations others set; add to this internalization the educational and legal constructs that make it harder for young Black males to avoid falling prey to negative projections.

Clearly the effects of internalized oppression continue to trouble Black America as is evidenced by Black-on-Black crime and the lack of support often provided in our communities for the prisoner, the homeless, and others who are struggling. Though many Blacks have managed to create a life of reasonable stability in our country, the reality of living where a race-based assault can occur at any time has its impact upon the overall well-being of the entire group.

It is clear to me that one of the tasks that Blacks have in the racial healing project is to understand this dynamic, learning not to accept the projections of others upon themselves nor engage in passing them along. In order to overcome internalized oppression, one must be vigilant. Without an understanding that the process is occurring, the challenges are more difficult. Internalized oppression does more than make us feel badly about ourselves; it causes great damage to the soul and psyche. It can also lead to a deep sense of rage as we are experiencing now.

The Rebirth of Black Rage

In 1966, when psychiatrists William Grier and Price Cobbs published *Black Rage*, there was no reason to believe that, almost five decades later, we would be experiencing the expression of black rage as we are today. Grier and Cobbs said, "Black rage is the result of our failure, after three hundred plus years to make it possible for Blacks to find a sense of identity, a sense of self-worth, to relate to others, to love, to work and to create." And they continued saying,

> People bear all they can and if required bear even more. But, if they are in present-day America they have been asked to shoulder too much. They will be harried no more. Turning from their tormentors, they are filled with rage.[1]

This is the result of a democracy defaulting on the promise to assure all its citizens the opportunity to achieve a level of success that supports a sense of self-worth and personal autonomy. Along with this, every citizen must believe that there is a collective concern for their safety and security. Young Black people cannot believe that in our society. While

1 William Grier, and Price Cobbs, *Black Rage* (New York: Basic Books, 1966), 4.

young people seem to be more at risk, it is clear that all Black people and persons of color are vulnerable to the powers that prevail. Their lives are minimized as deaths at the hands of enforcers of the law can attest. Whatever sense of security was gained as Jim Crow laws were dismantled has been completely eroded. Most Black parents live with a sense of unease about the well-being of their children, especially their male children. The lack of jobs, mass incarceration, the death penalty, laws such as stop-and-frisk, and the evidence of police misbehavior leveled at Black people serve to make the conversation on race more difficult than it would be if these things were not happening. Many of the young Black people with whom I have spoken can't imagine an honest conversation with a White person that will lead to positive changes for their lives. There is a sense of abandonment; for these young people, it seems clear that until and unless they take matters into their own hands, nothing is going to be done that will have any impact upon their lives.

In some ways this new expression of rage is encouraging: a few years ago it appeared that the young folks of all colors had given up holding accountable those in power. It is inspiring to see young people on campuses willing to stand up and be counted as they make their perspectives known. There are activists emerging across the country in part as a result of the deaths of young people at the hands of the police. It appears that today's young activists intend that these deaths will not be in vain.

Rage can be frightening if improperly channeled and detrimental to the person in whose soul it resides. However, rage used as the fuel to propel a new movement across this land benefits us all. It is critical that those who consider themselves elders find ways to be supportive of this new group of young social activists; there are great benefits in the memory and skill of those who have gone before. To be most effective, elders will need to listen with an open mind and heart, hearing fully and willing to accept rather than reject differences in style and substance.

The reasons for rage are as prevalent today as they were in 1966 when Grier and Cobbs wrote their seminal work. For some, the Obama presidency has been a contributor to their rage and disappointment, not realizing that as the first Black president, he would face huge limiting obstacles. This presidency has been the most disrespected in the history of America. Even a casual observance of how this president and first family are treated confirms the ongoing devaluation of Black skin.

Time will show us where the new movement will take us, but this type of activism is crucial as a factor in addressing internalized oppression. In the final analysis, this is a discussion about heart-and-soul energy and the ways in which that energy can be dissipated or activated. Oppression depletes energy and activism adds to it. This can be seen easily in ordinary daily life: when a person wakes feeling down, the day can be improved by becoming active. Taking a walk, going for a swim, writing notes to someone who is ill, or making a pot of soup for a sick neighbor can shift the energy. So it is with the energy drain from oppression and rage and its source in feelings of helplessness and immobilization. Further, if the rage is not addressed, it becomes depression.

Based in White supremacy projections necessary to relieve the guilt of slavery and its accompanying violence, the denial of depression is a direct result of the narrative of the strong Black person who bears all things. This is especially true for Black women. After all, we were expected to be able to rise above our humanity and be strong. When Blacks internalize this projection of outsized strength, it can be impossible to pursue treatment for depression. This denial leads to addiction, expressions of violence, physical illness, and a generalized sense of powerlessness affecting both personal and collective quality of life.

The page needs to be turned. The mask needs to be pulled off. Mental health needs to be raised to a higher level in the liberation process; no one can be free as long as the truth of their soul's state is unrealized or unacknowledged. Internal brokenness cannot be covered while one pretends all is well; it becomes impossible to function while maintaining such denial. Black pain must be unmasked so genuine healing can occur.

Following the murders of the Charleston Nine, I listened with great horror to the positive responses to statements of forgiveness issued by the families of the victims. Of course I believe that forgiveness is important, but three days following the murder of a loved one will not be the day that it happens.

I understand what happened. To the White supremacy constructs at work in our society, forgiveness was the only acceptable emotion for Blacks to express. During slavery, Black people were not allowed to show signs of rage, indignation, or grief because of the prevailing myth of "happy darkies." Though Blacks have survived in this country because of the ability to sing the pain away with spirituals and the blues, making a way out of no way, we did much damage to our souls in the process. It was not possible to be honest about our emotions; as Janie says in *Their Eyes Were Watching God,* "I starched my face and went out."[2] We are a people who know how to maintain the well-worn mask of the starched face.

When slave families were torn apart, when family members were lynched, when wages were stolen during sharecropping, when the police kill our children, when innocent people are sent to prison or executed, when we become the victims of the society's hatred for the poor and all other types of trouble visit us, we starch our faces and go out. We wear the mask.

As a columnist for a local newspaper, I get a constant barrage from readers who wish to tell me what I should have said or what I must have meant to say in my columns.

When we tell our stories and share out thoughts and feelings, we do not want them edited by the White listener or anyone else for that matter. It is crucial for White people to become clearer about the difference between walking on the path with someone and controlling the other's experience. Empathy is the ability to walk with another in full solidarity and appreciate the journey without commentary or editing.

Racial Healing for Black People

Clearly racism has damaged both Blacks and Whites. It is important for Black people to pay attention to how we have been wounded by systemic racism. It is understandable that we do not wish to be painted with a single brush, but what Joy DeGruy calls "post traumatic slave syndrome" seems to be quite true.[3] The suffering that came from the Middle Passage and life in North America cannot be erased from the collective consciousness in a few centuries.

When we look at the plight of the descendants of the slaves in this century, there are too many in prison, too many living in poverty and without access to high quality education or health insurance. We find that there is an ongoing assault upon the voting rights and other civil rights legislation which were passed in the 1960s. None of us who were working fifty years ago in that amazing movement for civil and human rights would have guessed that so much of the same work would be required today. The New Jim Crow argues that nothing short of a human rights movement rooted in the recognition of the basic dignity and humanity of all of us has any hope of ending mass incarceration

---

2   Zora Neale Hurston, *Their Eyes Were Watching God* (New York: Harper and Row, 1990), 84.

3   Joy DeGruy, *Post Traumatic Slave Syndrome* (Portland, OR: DeGruy Publications, 2005).

and dismantling the caste system in the United States.[4] This powerful assertion seems rooted in reality when one reviews the historical patterns regarding racial awakening and reform. W. E. B. DuBois once said that "the slave went free; stood a brief moment in the sun; then moved back again toward slavery[5] Clearly slaves were not aiming to become slaves again, but the circumstances of their lives recreated the conditions from which they had escaped for a brief moment.

What is required for the descendants of the slaves and the few free people who came to America from Africa to find a lasting freedom? It seems that the answer to this question is multilayered. I believe that it includes activism along with deep inner transformation.

There is no substitute for engaging the deep inner work that needs to be done. If there is excessive rage or depression, it needs to be addressed with the aid of a trained professional. Every effort needs to be made to discern the effects of internalized oppression. The daily onslaught of racism cannot be ignored. Black people should be encouraged to take the time needed to reflect upon the pain of the slights and injustices inflicted upon them each day. All of the possible resources—prayer, spiritual practice, therapy support groups, physical fitness activity, artistic expression, and a deep commitment to one's self—must be engaged. These are needed not to succumb to bitterness and unappropriated rage.

The line from *Their Eyes Were Watching God* rings so clearly: the primary character, Janie, says, "I learned that I had an inside and outside and I would never let them meet."[6]

How can one do that in a world that demands allegiance to its constructions and convention? It is a complicated matter to find one's spiritual and psychological core in the first place; many Black people have been so wounded by racism that the search cannot begin. So what can help?

Specific Strategies

For adults, the process toward becoming free of White supremacy's projections includes the exploration of what is crucial for your life. What are the things that make you vibrant and help you to embrace life with enthusiasm and purpose? This is a solo task, requiring the willingness to be honest and to listen to one's own heart. It is necessary

---

4   Michelle Alexander, *The New Jim Crow* (New York: New Press, 2010).

5   Ibid., 20.

6   Hurston, *Their Eyes Were Watching God*, 72.

to find space and time to be quiet, to get away from the noise of the phone, computer, other people, work, and social media. The clearing of the pollution of extraneous noise is critical to hear the still, quiet voice of God and of one's own heart.

Since oppression, just as racism is for Whites, is the sea that Blacks swim in, it is difficult to notice when and where it enters our lives at times. Some behaviors simply seem to be the way it is to be a person of color in the world rather than the result of long-term imprinting. When a Black person begins to make negative projections onto other Black people that mirror the ones that Whites have made onto Blacks, it is clearly a sign of having internalized the negative stereotyping. Occasionally Blacks will make the same projections onto other marginalized people as have been made on Blacks. It is impossible not to learn what one lives. The first step, then, is the determination to walk a different path. This intention will help to call attention to the times when the negative thoughts present themselves.

Black people have to explore the kinds of counterprojections that are made by them onto White people as well. There is no room for generalizing; it is a process fraught with fallacy. Though patterns can be seen in human behavior, they cannot become the primary method for understanding any group of people.

Let me be very clear at this point: this discussion is not about challenging every Black person to find a White person to befriend. This is a discussion about what may be necessary for Black people to more fully heal from the wounds of racism. Befriending and developing relationships with Whites will emerge after the inner work has been embraced. The possibility of genuine relationships will be greatly increased by this work. Guardedness and projections about Whites stand in the way of any type of connection beyond the superficial. The best antidote is self-awareness, which leads to being self-assured. There is no cure for the internalization of oppression except the discovery of one's own self and coming to see the worthy person who lives in your Black body.

Dr. Martin Luther King Jr. was right: our liberation is linked. White people must see themselves in a more true light, just as Blacks must. A new dialogue has to begin between individuals who refuse to live without authenticity. This process of projecting comes from what C. G. Jung characterized as *the shadow*, the part of the human being that holds things hidden from the person himself or herself; there is work that can be done to uncover those hidden parts.

Black people have hidden parts of their psyches just as Whites do. I was deeply troubled by some of my graduate school professors who wondered if I could apply Jungian principles to Black people. Jung was a theorist working and writing about universals, yet these highly educated liberal faculty folks were worried that Blacks would not be encompassed by a theory touting a universal collective consciousness. How racist of them.

Every individual is connected on this planet and we hold many things in common. Healing will come when we see that, as Black people, we can move beyond projecting onto Whites, understanding that no individual is better or worse than anyone else on the earth no matter the cultural constructs. Until the healing is accomplished, there will be no liberation. Black people do not have the luxury of waiting until the last racist dies to seek healing. Black life is too important to be put on hold waiting for the total destruction of racism. How can one work for healing when the wounding tools have not been destroyed? It is not easy, but it is crucial. Returning again to Thurman, it is important to define one's self in terms that do not give power to the external constructs that control and oppress.

Black people have to create a new identity. We have to separate ourselves from the world that has been created for us to inhabit. We must tell our stories in ways that make sense to us, to reclaim the best elements from our collective and personal histories, untainted by White supremacy's constructed reality. We have to recommit ourselves to the long and noble journey of building a new world: a world where masks are torn off and true emotions are experienced without shame; a world that aligns priorities for every person to have what is needed to live with quality and a sense of well-being on this planet; a world that looks beyond the color of a person's skin to see the face of God; a world that supports life; a world that will not be reduced to the control of greed; a world that will not settle for anything less than complete liberation; a world where no parent will hear their child say, "It is hard to be Black in America." This work will lead us home to ourselves and to true freedom. It will lead to healing for Blacks and Whites.

Diary of a Spoiled White Guy

Don Mosley

 "**D**onald Fred,**"** my father shouted at me, *"you have embarrassed me right in front of the biggest customer I have in the whole country! If you* ever *pull a stunt like that again, I'll . . . I'll . . ."* Dad's face was bright red as he groped for words. And then he realized that others had stopped their own conversation to listen, so I never learned just what punishment might await me.

It was 1954. We were in Birmingham, Alabama. My father, two of his salesmen, and I had come from our home in Waco, Texas, to visit a large scrap yard. Acres of land were piled high with old car bodies waiting to be crushed, sheared, and baled by large machines manufactured in Dad's factory, Mosley Machinery Company. The owner of the yard was making lots of money as he raced to keep up with the demand of the steel mills around Birmingham. The more his business grew, the more Mosley equipment he ordered.

Now he was considering another large expansion, so Dad agreed to come to Alabama to discuss what new machinery might be best. I was fifteen years old and I jumped at the chance to take the extra seat in our private plane and come along for the ride. The owner of the scrap yard met us at the airport and then proudly led us on a walking tour of his huge operation.

As we walked past some of the buildings, I noticed that the restrooms and the water fountains were boldly labeled "COLORED" or "WHITE."

I had seen such things before, of course, but (not being terribly interested in the adults' discussion about business matters) I began to wonder
whether there really might be some difference in the water in those
fountains.

In full view of the others, I marched over to one of the fountains
marked "COLORED" and tried it out. Hmm. No difference that I could
detect.

But when I turned back to the other men, I detected a big difference. All four of them were staring at me, aghast. My father, in particular, looked like he was about to have a stroke! He came over to me and
pulled me away from the fountains as he began to lecture me about what
a stupid thing I had done—but when he realized that the others were
watching us intently, he fell silent and led me back toward the group. I
knew there was much more to be heard once we got to the privacy of our
motel room that evening. And there was!

I want to emphasize here that my father was not a bad man at all.
To the contrary, I believe that he was an extraordinarily *good* man. I
could give a hundred examples of his love, his generosity to all kinds of
people, his faith in God, and his creative genius which allowed him and
my mother to climb out of extreme poverty and to achieve things beyond
the imagination of most of their peers. But, like most of the other people
around me as I grew up, he accepted without question the notion that
White people had been created at least a tad superior to Black people.
Here and there one might find exceptions, of course, but they were
simply that—exceptions to the general rule of things.

After I got my severe scolding back at the motel, my father gradually
began to calm down. Finally we joined his two salesmen and had supper
together in the restaurant downstairs. Afterward we stepped outside to
stroll around in the fresh air and to check on something in our rental car.
One of the salesmen said, "It's too early to hit the sack yet. Why don't we
drive around for a few minutes and see the exciting city of Birmingham?"

Just at that moment there was a loud explosion. It seemed to come
from over in the neighborhood near the scrap yard we had visited in the
afternoon. "Let's go see what happened!" our salesman friend shouted,
and minutes later we were racing back in that direction. Soon it became
obvious that we had done a stupid thing. We found ourselves in a neighborhood full of people—most of them Black—running in all directions.
At one point there were so many that we had to come to a full stop to
avoid running over someone. I saw a man throw a large rock, and then
we saw what looked like National Guardsmen begin to fire their guns

into the air and shout for people to go home. One of the salesmen yelled, "We've got to get out of here!"

Eventually we made it back to our motel. The next day we found only vague reports in the newspaper about an explosion of some kind that had triggered a brief riot. We never learned more than that, but what became clearer over the years that followed was that we had witnessed just a sample of the rising tensions and fear of many poor people in Alabama.

After that brief trip to Alabama, I began to listen with greater interest to reports about such events. Among other things, a young pastor named Dr. Martin Luther King Jr. began to make the news the following year as the leader of a bus boycott in Montgomery. Most of the reports I saw about such matters were quite negative, with some of them even accusing Dr. King of being a "communist agitator."

Meanwhile, I finished my high school education in an all-White public school, despite the fact that the Supreme Court had ordered an end to school segregation almost three years earlier. I had few conversations or other contacts with Black people, except with our house maids, Mandy and Vashti—and with the Black men who made up perhaps 10 percent of my father's employees. These were all very friendly people. They were also people who took care always to be polite and to "stay in their place," as I heard White people express it. The fact was, of course, that they had no choice about such matters if they wanted to keep their jobs and feed their children.

I see now that I was one of the most spoiled and coddled beneficiaries of the whole racist system. I shudder to think of the life of privilege and exploitation I might have lived at the expense of others if God had not had mercy and begun to open my eyes!

I was headed for some dramatic changes in my life. I now believe that one of the biggest reasons for those changes was the church which dominated so much of our family's time and energy. Sadly, it was not that the message of God's love for all people came to me through that church—but rather something close to the opposite of that.

I will not name the church or even the denomination with which it was affiliated, but what I experienced there was very different from the gospel that I believe Jesus actually taught and exemplified. The message I heard year after year was about the horrors of hell that awaited most people and about a God full of anger rather than of love. Along with the hellfire-and-brimstone message were those of militarism and racism as well—sometimes even including the "N" word used right from the pulpit!

I loved my parents and didn't want to hurt them by rejecting the church to which they belonged, but by the time I was in my mid-teens I was determined to find a way to escape this atmosphere of religious violence. I began to save money and to make plans for an extended trip away from home. Their tearful pleas delayed my departure briefly, but when I reached the age of twenty-one, I took off.

I crossed the Atlantic by ship, pedaled across Europe on a bicycle, and hitchhiked around the Middle East, determined to stretch my limited funds as far as possible. This was 1960, and I managed for five months to travel and live on an average of less than a dollar a day. In the process, I had some of the most life-changing experiences that one could imagine. Adventure followed exciting adventure, but the most important thing was that I shared life with poor people everywhere—refugees, war victims, people in all kinds of desperate situations that I could hardly have imagined back in my own life of privilege.

Just as I was feeling ready to burst with all of these new insights, I arrived at Assiout, Egypt. A few years earlier I had heard about an extraordinary woman there, Lillian Trasher, who had left her home in southern Georgia half a century earlier, when she was my age. Missionaries had taken her into their church compound in Upper Egypt, but when Lillian discovered hungry Egyptian orphans living in the street near the church, they refused to let her bring those children into the compound as well. So Lillian moved out to be with the children! Local Egyptians were so impressed by the courage and compassion of this young American woman that they began to contribute food and financial support to help her and the children.

By the time I arrived, exactly fifty years after her arrival late in 1910, Lillian had been "Mama" to more than 5,000 Egyptian orphans. Moreover, I found this seventy-six-year-old lady to be the perfect model of the joyful and loving Christianity that I had been missing in my church back in Waco, Texas. For two incredibly rich days I got to talk with her and eat my meals with her, watch hundreds of smiling children crowd as closely as possible around her—and see God's love being reflected through her to everyone she met.

I was profoundly affected by this experience—so much so that I returned to the United States and became one of the first people to apply to President Kennedy's brand new Peace Corps. I saw this as my own opportunity to go out and live among people very different from myself and—in a small way, at least—maybe to help others as Lillian Trasher had helped so many in Egypt.

Sure enough, I was assigned to work in a village in the jungles of

Malaysia. I was the lone White guy in a village of nearly 4,000 Malays, Indians, and Chinese. Furthermore, the Malays were all Muslims, the Indians all Hindus, and the Chinese all Buddhists and Baha'is. Where in all the earth could I have found a collection of people more different from the ones in my segregated White neighborhood back in Texas?

The next two years were full of profound and enriching cross-cultural experiences, one after another. I developed a large circle of friends with many different skin colors, languages, and religions. I began to realize how often I had dealt with other people as stereotypes instead of recognizing each of them as unique individuals. I learned to see the world through their eyes. I began to develop new insights about things like international politics, economics, and God's incredibly rich variety of children.

Among other things, I began to see the tremendous economic and military power of the United States from the perspectives of other people around the world. This was especially evident as I studied the growing conflict just a few hundred miles away in Vietnam.

I also saw what was happening back in my own country through new lenses, most all the reports about the civil rights movement. The march from Selma to Montgomery took place during my final months in Malaysia. Halfway around the world, I was deeply moved by the courage and the eloquence of Dr. Martin Luther King Jr. I began to wonder what I should do in response to these events.

I returned home late in 1965. My father's business was booming, and for the next few months he tried desperately to persuade me to set aside these other interests and to start assuming the leadership of Mosley Machinery Company. I had majored in mechanical engineering in college and had already worked on a part-time basis with the company for several years. Here was my chance to become a millionaire businessman and. . . .

Somehow that just didn't fit with the larger set of concerns that had begun to dominate my thinking, concerns about how to help promote peace and justice in a world where I had discovered so much violence, injustice, and suffering—much of it caused by racism and other distorted views of our neighbors on this small planet we share.

While I struggled with these painful decisions, I fell in love with a very smart and very beautiful young woman. Luckily she was also crazy enough that she agreed to marry me. Then we began to pray together and struggle with the question of what we should do next. Finally, Carolyn and I decided that I should accept the offer of another round of service in the Peace Corps in Asia.

Our parents were dismayed, of course, but our family bonds of love remained strong. They saw us off to South Korea with tears in their eyes and the hope that this time we'd finally "get it out of our system" and come back to Waco permanently.

I became the supervisor of more than a hundred Peace Corps Volunteers in Seoul and across the northern third of South Korea. Those lively PCVs, most of them only slightly younger than I was, worked as English teachers and as assistants in rural health departments. Most of them were assigned to jobs in remote villages and small towns just south of the DMZ at a time of extremely high tension between North Korea and the joint forces of South Korea and the United States. (At one point Carolyn and I were trapped inside a building with a large crowd of the volunteers while a battle took place in the forest all around us, leaving almost a hundred North and South Korean soldiers dead.) Month after month I drove my jeep from one volunteer site to another, checking on their safety and their job performance. I also attended confidential briefings at the US Embassy. Among other things, these briefings made it very clear to me how easy it would be for the tensions to escalate into an all-out war, one which could readily lead to the use of some of the nuclear weapons we all knew to be waiting not far away.

Is it any wonder that I began to take an intense interest in every report I found concerning Martin Luther King's prophetic statements about such matters? He had given his historic speech at Riverside Church, "Beyond Vietnam—A Time to Break Silence," the week before Carolyn and I were married. Many of the volunteers I was now supervising had been active protesters back in the States against that war, and now the United States was paying thousands of poor people from South Korea to fight as mercenaries in Vietnam. All of this was at the same time war was threatening to escalate dramatically on the Korean Peninsula itself.

Among other things, Dr. King was helping this White guy to recognize a relationship between war and racism that I might never have figured out without his eloquence. Certainly one factor common to both was the practice of looking on large numbers of people as far less than unique and loveable individuals created by God. Instead, they were seen as expendable masses, often pitted against each other, frequently becoming the targets of bullets and bombs.

I was chosen to give a speech one evening in the spring of 1968. The audience was made up mostly of Korean officials, including one of the most powerful members of President Pak Chung Hee's inner staff. I was asked to speak about the objectives of the Peace Corps around the world, especially in South Korea. Needless to say, I was pretty nervous as I hastily prepared my notes for the presentation.

Just an hour or two before the speech, I learned of Martin Luther King's assassination. I was shocked, but I knew what I had to do: I threw away my notes and spoke instead about the power of nonviolence, about the way Dr. King had demonstrated so convincingly that "only love can drive out hate!" I don't know whether I convinced anyone—I can still remember a room full of rather noncommittal stares as I spoke—but I like to think that one of heaven's newest arrivals was looking down on us with a smile of approval.

A few weeks later I received a package from a friend in the United States who was struggling with many of the same issues that I was. I opened the box and found a dozen large reels of tape recordings. As I listened to them, I was amazed. It was my introduction to Dr. Clarence Jordan and the dramatic story of Koinonia Farm in southwest Georgia. Here was a man with a PhD in Greek, a New Testament scholar with impressive academic credentials and a passion for discerning what the teachings of Jesus and the testimony of the early Christian communities, known as "koinonias" in Greek, should mean in today's world. More than that, he and a small group of courageous friends were boldly putting those insights into action in daily life in a racially integrated Christian community.

Clarence traveled and spoke in many churches, conferences, and other settings about the evils of racism, military violence, and material greed. He had a huge impact on many audiences with his combination of eloquence and humor. Drawing constantly from his expert knowledge of the original Greek biblical texts, he applied the teachings to modern life in the situations right around him in south Georgia, to life "in the cotton patch." Clarence and the others at Koinonia were doing their best to go beyond mere words. *They were putting those teachings of Jesus into action!*

Following the example of the earliest churches, the people of Koinonia Farm took a strong stand against military violence and echoed Jesus's teaching that we should *love* all of our "enemies," whether nearby or far away. They also followed the example of those first Christians and pooled their personal belongings, living from a "common purse" financially. Most provocative, as it turned out, was the fact that they welcomed people into their circle without regard to race, joyfully sharing meals and worship services with each other.

As a result, they were excluded from local churches, their farm products were boycotted, and many local merchants refused to do business with them at all. Night riders began to fire guns at them and even to dynamite their buildings! Year after year the pressures grew, until some of the families could take no more. They began to pack up and move away. By the latter part of the 1960s there were only a handful of residents left at Koinonia. Even Clarence Jordan himself was beginning to question whether the time had come to sell out and move to a new location.

Millard and Linda Fuller had visited Koinonia in 1964. They were struggling with major problems in their own lives, and they decided almost on a whim to swing by Koinonia to visit an old friend, Al Henry, for an hour or two. Al introduced them to Clarence Jordan—and their visit stretched to a full month! Over the next few years they remained in touch, and in July of 1968 the Fuller family moved to Koinonia.

With the arrival of the Fullers, something beautiful and powerful began to unfold. Both families, the Jordans and the Fullers, had been searching for new direction in their lives. They became a powerful team as they searched together, Clarence's faith and knowledge of the Bible being joined by Millard's astounding energy and creativity.

In August 1968 they called together a dozen friends from all over the country and spent three days in intensive, prayerful searching for new ways of responding to the racism, poverty, and violence that permeated the world around them, near and far. (It was one of these participants, Ladon Sheats, who sent the tape recordings to us in South Korea and drew us into the excitement.) Out of that three-day conference came a new vision that has since affected the lives of countless people around the world.

The theme of "partnership" was emphasized, "partnership with God and with people everywhere," as Clarence put it. The goal should be to create new relationships and structures that would allow people of many backgrounds to work *together* to overcome the problems that had been created by segregation, poverty, and other aspects of racism. The community's name was formally changed from "Koinonia Farm" to "Koinonia Partners," and the "Fund for Humanity" was established to help finance the new ventures.

One of the most obvious consequences of the intense racism in the region was that most of the poverty-stricken Black families lived in dilapidated houses, shacks that were often in worse condition than the barns and chicken houses owned by their White neighbors. Impossible to heat adequately in the winter, infested with rats, these old sharecroppers' houses were no place to raise little children. Yet there were scores of such shacks within a few miles of Koinonia.

Thus it was that the group of dreamers who gathered at Koinonia in 1968 came up with a wonderfully ambitious idea—"partnership housing," a program that would provide modest new houses at a price that even the poor neighbors could afford. Twenty-five acres of Koinonia's land was divided into half-acre housing lots with a spacious park in the middle. Hundreds of friends on the Koinonia mailing list contributed to the Fund for Humanity, and construction of the first half dozen houses was begun by local contractors.

Meanwhile, over in South Korea, by the time I had listened to all those tape recordings a couple of times, I was hooked. I began to explore the possibility of visiting Koinonia. Carolyn was open to the idea but had serious doubts, thanks largely to the fact that we now had a cute little baby boy whose safety had to be taken into consideration as well. After a while we agreed that we should spend at least a few weeks there, and then we could decide whether to stay longer. I was looking forward very much to talking with Clarence.

Sadly, my conversation with Clarence was not to be. Late in 1969, just as we were moving back to the United States after more than two years in Korea, we got news that Clarence had died suddenly of a heart attack. Nevertheless, we continued to make plans for an exploratory visit to Koinonia.

When we arrived there in June of 1970, we found a beehive of activity. When Carolyn and I walked into the front office, we were warmly welcomed by a young woman, Mildred Burton, with a big smile and a hearty shout of "WELCOME TO KOINONIA!" Within a minute or two, we were being hugged by others in the office, Black people and White people who made it very obvious that we had just discovered a place where love was far more important than things like race or other minor differences between people.

Hearing the commotion in the front office, Millard Fuller came rushing in and added his enthusiastic greetings. There is no way on earth that I could have foreseen what life-changing adventures lay ahead in my friendship with this tall, smiling man who was pumping my hand as though he had been eagerly awaiting my arrival for years.

The welcomes continued for almost an hour, and then we were escorted to our new living quarters. At first we were a bit nervous to find that we were going to occupy the little house right by the front entrance, less than a hundred feet from Georgia Highway 49. Indeed, as I walked around during the next few days when I had the opportunity, I found at least a dozen bullet holes in the gas pump and other structures near our house—messages of hate from the KKK and others who had cruised back and forth along that highway at night during the past few years.

As it turned out though, we could hardly have arrived at a more opportune time. Not only did our arrival coincide with the end of such violent attacks on the community, but the air at Koinonia was full of excitement and new vision. The office had just been expanded. The pecan shelling plant was working at full speed to keep up with orders that were pouring in daily. A team of cooks produced fruit cakes and chocolate pecan candy, while another team worked as fast as they could to box the products and get them loaded into the delivery trucks each day.

All of this was the tangible result of Koinonia's new drive to combat poverty and racism by creating programs designed to provide employment for neighbors who needed jobs, better schools for all children regardless of race, decent houses to live in—and to do so joyfully as a way to put their faith in God into actual practice.

Over and over I heard Clarence Jordan's famous declaration that "faith is not belief in spite of evidence but a life in scorn of the consequences!" What I saw unfolding around me was the result of a small group of faithful Christians, Black and White, who had defied the bullets and the threats of hostile neighbors, determined to live faithfully by Jesus's teachings whatever the consequences might be.

Carolyn and I spent an exciting summer at Koinonia, returned to Texas for a few months while I finished an MA degree, and then moved back to Koinonia for what was to be almost a decade full of some of the richest experiences of our lives.

Among the most important of those experiences were the many loving friendships with our neighbors without regard for racial backgrounds. The majority of our closest neighbors were Black families with whom we worked, worshiped, and celebrated together the rich life God had given us. Forty years later, I still love to think of our warm friendships with our neighbors—Mamie, Bo, Mattie Lee, Mildred, Ludrell, Perry, Doris, Emma, Ethel . . . the list goes on and on. (And I remember some rich discussions with one bright young lady who didn't live at Koinonia but was a frequent visitor—named Catherine Meeks—later to become the same Dr. Catherine Meeks who has called us together to write this book!)

I had worked with my father's company as an engineer for a few years, but I had never built a house. I was fascinated by the new housing project, and I loved working with the professional contractors who visited Koinonia to help with the construction.

I was completely surprised, however, when Millard walked up to me one day and announced, "Don, I want you to be the director of our partnership housing program!" When I caught my breath, I told him that I was not at all qualified to do such a thing, that I was still learning the basics.

"Don't worry. You'll learn fast from all of these contractors and other folks who are helping us." Sure enough, I did—and so did the growing team of young volunteer workers who made up most of my work crews. Within a year we were turning out new houses at the rate of one a month.

The cost of the houses was kept to a minimum by relying almost totally on volunteer work crews, by providing the lots free of charge (as part of a community land trust), and by requiring each new homeowner to help with the construction for a certain number of hours, referred to as their "sweat equity." In the 1970s, that made it possible for us to turn out a new house with two or three bedrooms for about $6,000 each, to be paid off in 20 years with no charge for profit or for interest on the loan. Even the poorest families could usually afford house payments of $25 a month. These monthly payments then went back into the Fund for Humanity to help finance future homes.

For me, one of the richest parts of the whole process was the experience of working side by side with the new homeowners and their families. In this way I came to know dozens of new families well, people who were very excited to be moving from collapsing shacks into solid, attractive new houses. I was working essentially as a volunteer myself, but I wouldn't have traded this job for one with a huge salary elsewhere.

It was during this exciting period in the early 1970s that I took a member of our Koinonia Board of Directors for a walking tour of the project. His name was Tom Boone, a lively descendent of pioneer Daniel Boone's brother half a dozen generations back. As I showed him our new houses and described the many friendships that were developing as we worked alongside people who had been living in poverty, Tom responded with one of the most profound statements I had ever heard.

"Don," he said, "People *act* their way into new ways of thinking far more often than they *think* their way into new ways of acting."

I am convinced that Tom Boone's statement applies to the challenge of overcoming racism as much as to any other problem in life. Thinking is essential, of course, but for most of us it is only when we get out and *meet* people and *apply* our new ideas that we really begin to connect the dots and grasp realities which might well have remained abstractions for us otherwise.

Millard Fuller often referred to the "theology of the hammer," and we were pounding those hammers at a rapidly increasing rate. After we had completed the first two dozen houses at Koinonia, the Fullers moved to Mbandaka, Zaire (now Republic of the Congo), in central Africa. Millard and I had been brainstorming about how to spread this new vision, and late in 1973 he asked me to come help him launch a similar project on the banks of the Congo River. I spent the month of January, 1974, surveying the lots for 110 houses and helping to start the construction on the first ones.

The project was located in the middle of Mbankaka on a large block of open land that the white Belgian colonialists had preserved as the "sanitation strip" intended to separate their own houses along the river from those of the black Africans on the other side of the strip. Millard and I happily chose it from the three sites offered by the local officials of Zaire (the Belgians having left more than a decade earlier when Zaire gained its independence).

Millard had already established a close friendship with one of the local church leaders, Pastor Boyaka Inkomo. When we told him where we were planning to start the housing project, he seemed quite surprised at first—and then he got a big smile on his face.

"You know what we call that piece of land in Lingala, don't you?" he asked. When we said no, he explained, "It is known by all people here as 'Bokotola.' In Lingala that means 'a person who does not like others.'"

When the time came for Millard and Linda to leave Mbandaka in mid-1976, there were 114 houses either completed and occupied or under construction. There was a huge celebration, in which the name was formally changed from "Bokotola" to "Losanganya"—the Lingala word meaning "reconciler, reunifier, everyone together."

Racism had just been dealt a powerful blow!

When the Fullers returned to the United States, I was serving as director of Koinonia. Millard was wildly enthusiastic about the way the work had gone in Zaire, and he was convinced that this model would work in other countries as well. He proposed that we call together another group of friends, as he and Clarence Jordan had done in 1968, to pray and search together for a vision of how this might be repeated in many other places. I agreed immediately, and we decided to meet for three days at Koinonia in a room that had been upgraded recently from its earlier use as a chicken house.

Twenty-seven people came together, black and white, local and from around the United States. One man, Mompongo Mo Imana, came all the way from Mbandaka, Zaire, to share in this envisioning process.

Beginning September 24, 1976, we met for three days in that simple little building and discussed the exciting things that had already taken place and prayed for God to show us how to reach even more families needing decent housing.

Hundreds of people at Koinonia and in Africa, mostly children, had already been helped by our combined efforts. All of us in that room agreed that improved housing was an important achievement, but in the process we had discovered something else at least as important as the housing itself. That was the fact that, as we had worked together for justice in housing for these families we had also found a wonderful way to build loving friendships and overcome racism as well.

Now we were daring to dream that we might be able to start something that could eventually help *thousands* of people in new locations. Who knows where this thing might lead to if we worked at it hard enough? Millard, always out at the leading edge of such thinking, actually suggested to the rest of us that our efforts might help a *million* people someday. Needless to say, that was a bit beyond most of our imaginations.

By the end of the meeting, a name had been chosen: we had just launched "Habitat for Humanity." If any of us in that room, even Millard, had been able to see forty years into the future—when, in fact, over a million homes have been built in thousands of projects around the globe, bringing together many millions of workers from every conceivable ethnic and cultural background—the reality is that we couldn't have wrapped our minds around such a vision.

Hey, Tom, you're right! People do act their way into new ways of thinking!

As it happens, a neighbor eight miles up the road from Koinonia was discovering the same thing and making headlines in the process. A few years earlier Jimmy Carter had entered politics by being elected to the Sumter County Board of Education. He had grown up in the county (which also contains Koinonia and the city of Americus), but he was shocked to observe firsthand the extreme racism of some of the members of the Board of Education. Forced by the Supreme Court to admit black students into the county's public schools, several of the BOE members had pulled their own children out of the schools and enrolled them in segregated "Christian academies" in the area. They served on the Board of Education not to improve the education for the others but to keep the level of taxation and funding for public schools at the lowest possible level.

Jimmy Carter decided to try to fight against this racist system at a higher level, so he left the Board of Education and ran successfully for the Georgia State Legislature. In 1970, just as Carolyn and I were arriving at Koinonia, Carter was launching his successful campaign to be governor of Georgia. His strong commitment to human rights for all people became a trademark of his career as he continued to climb up the political ladder.

As it happens, we were praying and dreaming in that fancied-up chicken house at Koinonia in the fall of 1976—starting Habitat for Humanity—just five weeks before our neighbor was elected to be *President* Jimmy Carter.

With our own Koinonia children, Black and White, attending the local public schools, we had become increasingly concerned about the same racist policies that had launched Jimmy Carter's political career. Carolyn became the president of the PTA at the Plains Elementary School. The Carters' daughter, Amy, was a student during that time, and I sometimes helped the Secret Service man with childcare at the playground while Jimmy and Rosalynn were out of town on the campaign trail. In a meeting with other concerned parents, we founded the Sumter County Organization for Public Education (SCOPE). Our goal was to continue what Jimmy Carter had been doing a few years earlier: counter the intense racism of the Board of Education. I attended the BOE meetings each month, ignored their scowls of anger, and reported their blatant racism (racist jokes and all) to the local newspapers. I managed to get a television crew into Plains High School during a rainstorm, and that night the evening news showed the water pouring through the dilapidated roof of the school and splattering on the desks of the students during their classes.

The other rural high school in Sumter County was in the small town of Leslie. It was in even worse condition, with the central auditorium having literally collapsed into a pile of rubble. Meanwhile, the students had to attend classes in the rooms that had not yet collapsed.

Rather than seeking funds to repair these deteriorating buildings, the BOE was doing the opposite. They were helping to block tax money from being used for these schools, even to the extent of refusing to accept funds that were available from the state of Georgia.

This became the primary focus of our SCOPE campaign. For almost a year we carried out an increasingly vigorous publicity campaign. Barely a month after arriving at the White House, President Carter helped us by recording a speech I wrote about the situation and his determination to fight against such despicable racist policies. It was played on the evening news, with the television camera showing the tape as the president's voice was broadcast. A short time later, twenty-seven SCOPE members went to court to try to force the BOE to repair or replace the dilapidated schools. "Don Mosley et al. vs. the Sumter County Board of Education" took months of court hearings and legal action, but finally we won. A large grant was awarded by the state of Georgia, and a new Sumter County Comprehensive High School was built for *all* students.

In April 1979, Koinonia gave birth to yet another new venture, Jubilee Partners. After many months of intensive preparation, three families moved to northeast Georgia and set up their tents on 260 acres of beautiful land. Carolyn and I had been thinking and praying for years about how we might expand Koinonia's work for peace and justice. We were joined by two other families, the Weirs and the Karises. (Ryan and Karen Karis had also gone to Zaire for several months and helped to expand Habitat's work to a new location, the village of Ntondo.)

We lived for many months in a cluster of tents in an open field and worked vigorously to get our first houses built before winter came. Once again, our empathy with the suffering of others was increased by our own temporary discomfort. As we struggled to build more substantial shelter for ourselves and our children, we became much more sensitive to the reports about the suffering of the refugees from the recent war in Vietnam.

By midsummer, we had made the decision to make Jubilee Partners a place where such refugees could come for relief and safety. As we began to describe that vision to others, we got an immediate surge of affirmation and encouragement. I met with refugee relief experts in New York and Atlanta, and all of them urged us to push ahead with our plans to develop a refugee orientation center at Jubilee.

When we announced our new vision in a newsletter, the very first response was one that I will treasure as long as I live. It was from Willie Mae Champion, a longtime friend at Koinonia, one who had, in fact, participated three years earlier in the meeting that gave birth to Habitat for Humanity. Willie Mae and I had worked together on one project after another to help people around Koinonia.

Now she was writing to tell me how thrilled she was to hear about our plans to help the suffering refugees. Having grown up in a poor sharecropper's shack, she had a special empathy for those refugees. She apologized that she had no money to send, but she assured us that she would be praying for our success in this great effort of compassion. "By their fruits, ye shall know them," she concluded.

We set ourselves a goal to try to be ready to receive the first refugees at Jubilee within one year. Never have I packed more hours of work into each day than during that year. All of us—along with many friends who joined us for up to weeks at a time—were determined to be ready to receive our first refugee guests as soon as possible.

Meanwhile, we were very pleased to hear President Carter's call for aid to such people. While we were building the first refugee cabins at Jubilee, he signed the Refugee Act of 1980 into law, dramatically increasing the number of refugees to be admitted into the United States each year. First Lady Rosalynn Carter actually went to the refugee camps in Southeast Asia and met some of the refugees face-to-face.

The head of the United Methodist refugee resettlement program called me from New York and asked if we would consider hosting two or three dozen Cuban refugees—men from the "Freedom Flotilla"—before we started working with the Vietnamese who had first caught our attention. We agreed at once, and a few days later I went to the Krome Detention Center near Miami to interview prospects for our new program.

I spent many hours listening to deeply moving stories from these men, all of whom were desperate to gain their freedom and to be able to continue with their lives. They were all shades of black, brown, and white, with a wild variety of mustaches and beards. Almost all of them had gotten into trouble with the Cuban government somehow and found ways to get to Florida. US officials had arrested thousands of them and put them into detention centers. After an exhausting day of interviews with the help of an official interpreter, I selected about three dozen men as candidates for our new program.

The very first man I selected was Rodolfo Portillo, a small man about fifty years old and as dark as ebony. He had come to the States in a desperate attempt to earn money to buy medicine for his wife, who was severely ill. His eyes suddenly filled with tears as he told me, "Yesterday I received word that I am too late. My wife has died." After an awkward pause, he continued, "But now, you see, it is more important than ever for me to get out of here so I can help my children."

I agreed, and thus it was that a few days later Rodolfo was one of fourteen men who climbed off a plane in Atlanta and became the first of what has since developed into a river of humanity flowing through our facilities and our little town of Comer, Georgia. Somewhere close to four thousand men, women, and children from three dozen countries have followed him through Jubilee's orientation and English language program since that time. Most of them have been in residence with us for about two months before moving to more permanent sites around the United States.

These courageous refugees have come to Jubilee from the worst disasters around the world. We are always inspired by them. There have been hundreds of stories of dramatic escape or other situations that could fill many books. Over and over again, their presence with us has inspired us to travel to the war zones ourselves to try to help others left behind. I've organized and led more than a dozen delegations to such places. Along the way we have launched relief efforts in Asia, Africa, and Central America to help those still suffering there.

Our greatest reward, whether in distant lands or back home at Jubilee, is the love we share with the beautiful children of this world. To love these children, to give them food and medicine and warm clothing, to smile into their little faces and receive their bright smiles in return—all of this is worth more than any amount of money could buy. To watch little kids from all corners of the world play together, hug each other, communicate amazingly well with the few words of English that they share in common . . . "Racism? What is that? Not on *our* playground!"

Trying to communicate some of what I have learned from these children and their parents, I have had the privilege of speaking to thousands of groups on campuses and in churches all over the United States and Canada, but never have I felt more honored than in the early 1980s when I was invited to preach at Dexter Avenue Baptist Church in Montgomery, Alabama. The pastor at that time was Dr. G. Murray Branch, a brilliant man who served on the Board of Directors of Habitat for Humanity and then that of Jubilee Partners. We were close friends, but still I was astounded when Murray invited me to come preach from the very pulpit from which Dr. Martin Luther King Jr. had preached for years in the late 1950s. I felt extremely inadequate for the task, but with a pounding heart I accepted the invitation.

Carolyn and I were Murray and Mima Branch's guests Saturday night in the church's parsonage on Jackson Street, the same house where Martin and Coretta and their children had lived during those tumultuous years of the Montgomery bus boycott that caught the attention of the world. After one of Mima's delicious meals (and I was privileged to enjoy many of them over the years), we went to our bedrooms to rest for the next day's events.

I could not sleep. I was too awed by the significance of what had happened in this parsonage. In particular, my mind kept going back to the story that King related in his book *Stride toward Freedom* about the evening in this same house when *he* could not sleep because of the weight of fear that came down on him as the bus boycott brought more and more threats against his life and his wife and little daughter.

I slipped out of bed and walked quietly into the dark kitchen. I thought about how King told about getting out of bed and coming into this same kitchen and praying, "I am here taking a stand for what I believe is right. But now I am afraid . . . I am at the end of my powers. I have nothing left. I've come to the point where I can't face it alone."

And then, he said, it had happened: "I experienced the presence of the Divine as I had never experienced Him before." King felt an assurance sweep over him that God would be at his side forever. "Almost at once my fears began to go. My uncertainty disappeared. I was ready to face anything." Even the bomb that was thrown onto the front porch of the parsonage three nights later—and the dangerous riot that was developing as hundreds of angry people gathered and were confronted roughly by heavily armed police. Drawing on the peace that had come to him that night in his kitchen, he stood on the porch beside the hole that just been blasted in it and shouted out his eloquent message of love and nonviolence. "If you have weapons, take them home. . . . We cannot solve this problem though retaliatory violence. We must meet violence with nonviolence. Remember the words of Jesus: 'He who lives by the sword will perish by the sword.' . . . We must love our white brothers."

God's miraculous love was communicated and demonstrated so well by that twenty-seven-year-old pastor that the crowd dispersed without a single person being injured—and the whole world began to realize that something beautiful and powerful was happening here in Montgomery.

In my sermon at Dexter Avenue, I expressed how unworthy I felt to stand in that pulpit but how eager I was to take the lessons I had learned from this congregation and their neighbors and put them into practice. I took Luke 19:42, "the way that leads to peace," as my text. I described the way their loving nonviolence had helped me to become more aware of my own racism and of my complicity with other forms of violence on many fronts.

Not long after that, I had the wonderful experience of a visit with Coretta Scott King. We talked especially about her memories of the bus boycott, a time when she and her young husband were not at all sure that they would survive the racist fury unleashed by the stand they were taking for justice. As we talked, it became very clear why Martin had often referred to her not only as his "beloved wife" but also as his "coworker."

Our work at Jubilee Partners with the refugees and our efforts at peacemaking in situations around the world have continued to deepen my confidence in the power of love put into action. Despite the widespread addiction to violence in our own society and far beyond, God continues to work through those who refuse to hate other people—whatever their differences in color, religion, politics, or anything else.

That is where I find my hope, however gloomy and threatening the evening news may become.

And that is why my favorite place now in all of Washington, DC, is that pretty little meadow beside the Tidal Basin, right between the statue of Dr. Martin Luther King Jr. and that gray marble wall inscribed with his words, "Darkness cannot drive out darkness, only light can do that. Hate cannot drive out hate, only love can do that."

Dear God, please help us to love each other more!

CHAPTER 6

A White Lens on Dismantling Racism

Diane D'Souza

It is in the ordinary that the extraordinary is revealed, and the ordinary does not begin in extraordinary ways. As we face down the plague of racism, poverty, and inequality, we are called by God to create revolutionary acts of change in often very ordinary ways. . . . And that is what's most extraordinary of all.

—Rev. Dr. Serene Jones[1]

I did not anticipate that writing this chapter would be so hard. I wanted to write about the concrete work of dismantling racism to encourage us when we despair that things will never change. Our keen focus on the things we need to fix sometimes blinds us to places where progress is being made. I also wanted to inspire action or potential direction among other Whites who sometimes wonder what part they can play in bringing change. I've seen individuals and church congregations become aware of the pervasive evil of racism and then get stalled on what they can do to uproot it. This chapter, I thought, could provide a few windows into the practical work of dismantling racism and building Beloved Community.

---

1   Serene Jones, "Sermon Four," in SELMA *Hand-in-Hand Sermon Guide* (Washington: Values Partnerships, 2015), 19.

Yet in the process of writing I learned how hard it is to separate my research and teaching from my own journey as a white Euro American[2] woman recovering from racism. In the course of talking with many people about their work of making change, I had an uncomfortable interaction that fueled significant personal growth. This experience was humbling and important, shedding light on the process of challenge and change inherent to dismantling racism. I realized it would be valuable to relate that story and what I learned from it, but struggled with how to do that authentically. In the United States it is normative to place White people's stories and feelings at the center of discourse. This is a norm I am committed to change. Using my own story to frame the chapter seemed to contradict what I believe. I also knew that I wanted to shine a strong light on the realities of racism—as do the three stories I chose to tell—since Whites often have the privilege of ignoring racial inequities. At the same time, relegating my personal experiences to a concluding footnote would mean readers might not understand my motivation in telling these stories. After months of wrestling with this question, and feedback from people I trust,[3] I finally decided that to accept Malcolm X's invitation to engage White communities around racism[4] meant that I needed to tell the truth about this messy, painful, and ultimately reconciling and healing process—even the struggle to value and find a place for our own stories.

The racism that is the focus of this chapter is a system of oppression that assigns privilege, respect, and value based on the whiteness of a person's skin. I join others in using the expression "dismantling racism" because it conveys that racism is not just about feelings and interpersonal relationships but also social institutions and systems that we have constructed, are complicit in maintaining, and must act intentionally to deconstruct. "Building Beloved Community" is the positive compass that helps orient our construction of a different reality.

---

2 Recognizing that every term has inherent limitations, I use the descriptors Euro American and Afro American to indicate United States citizens of European and African ancestry. They are interchangeable with White and Black. My preference for the prefix Afro draws on the endorsement of citizens of Caribbean background who find it more resonant than "African American." I value the term Euro American because it forces Whites to claim their ethnic identity alongside other US citizens, and also because it reminds us that every White American is also an immigrant.

3 Thank you to Ann Moritz, Abigail Ortiz, Donna Bivens, Noel D'Souza, Bennie Wiley, Bithiah Carter, and Mira D'Souza: this chapter is richer for your input. Any mistakes or shortcomings in its scope or content are my own.

4 "Let sincere white individuals find all other white people they can who feel as they do—and let them form their own all-white groups, to work trying to convert other white people who are thinking and acting so racist. Let sincere whites go and teach non-violence to white people!" Malcolm X, *The Autobiography of Malcolm X* (London: Penguin, 1965), 494–95.

I have come to think of racism as a soup we're all swimming in. Unlike the sea, a soup is created by human enterprise and its flavor and consistency are formed by the ingredients we add to it. Just as it is difficult to change the flavor of a broth once you have added too much salt or a strong spice, our racism soup resists change. Swimming in a broth created collectively over countless generations, we steep in toxic privilege and oppressive diminishment—even if we fail to see or acknowledge it. It does not matter whether we live in a mixed race community or a homogenous one, we all soak in this soup. As a person raised and living in the United States, racism enters and resides in me in ways I am mostly unaware of until I slam into it. Such encounters are painful, and yet they carry the seeds of transformation for, as James Baldwin reportedly observed, "You cannot fix what you cannot face." Forced to acknowledge my own racism, I can choose to respond differently from how it dictates. I can create a different mindset. I can reach out when my urge is to draw back. I can begin to shape a different future. To face and then reject the evil that infects me is to choose life, for the power of racism lies in alienating us from each other and from ourselves.

A Journey toward Wholeness

I grew up in a relatively homogenous town in New Jersey. In my high school, with the exception of one classmate who was Afro American, all students, staff, and faculty were of European descent. Like most middle- or upper-class White Protestant families, mine did not talk about race. It was in Montreal while attending graduate school that I met and married a fellow graduate student from India. My parents were not pleased with the union. Most hurtful was my father's lament, "I never thought I'd have brown grandchildren."

Being a partner to a non-American person of color opened my eyes to racism and xenophobia. I was nonplussed when Canadian immigration officials would not allow Andreas's brother to get a visa and come from India to attend our wedding. The skeptical official who interviewed us in Canada displayed a cavalier disrespect I had never encountered in my own interactions with government representatives. In a similar way, I had not given much thought to crossing the US–Canadian border. In six years of traversing it, I never associated my effortless crossing with my privilege as a White American. Then that privilege disappeared. I now had a new normal: longer stops to talk with border security guards about who we were and why we were traveling, and not infrequently being asked to park our car and go into the immigration office for a more detailed interview.

Indeed, the crossing of borders seems to be one of the places where racism becomes most visible. The most striking example for me was a trip we took to the United Kingdom. Walking to the immigration area through long airport hallways, we passed a group of several dozen South Asian people sitting on the floor. Except for their worn clothing, this waiting cluster of travelers did not look very different from my husband. When we reached the immigration check post, Andreas and I found ourselves going through separate lines, perhaps because of a delay due to a bathroom stop, or the need of one of our children, or because there were different queues for Indian and American passport holders. I don't remember the reason. What I do remember is hearing Andreas shout my name as I began to merge with the crowd of travelers newly admitted to the UK. Turning back I saw him still at the check post talking animatedly to one of the officers. He pointed to where I and our children stood yards away amidst a stream of other passengers. The official turned, looked at me for a long moment, then turned back to stamp my husband's passport. My Whiteness gave my brown husband a pass.

I learned more about racism, Whiteness, and what it feels like to be a visible minority by living and working in India for twenty years. India's legacy of colonialism also gave me a new window into White privilege. An early example occurred when I became sick and the lingering symptoms prompted my husband and me to look for a doctor. Following a neighbor's directions to a nearby clinic, we were surprised to find the waiting area full and a line of people snaking out into the courtyard. Preparing for a long wait, we were urged by one after another in the crowd to go to the front of the line. Feeling weak and unwell, I was troubled by this but grateful for people's generosity in letting a stranger see the doctor first. For me, this was an example of kindness and gracious hospitality. As I spent more time in India, though, I began to realize that Whiteness brought privilege even in a country where most people's bodies were brown or black. Had I been of dark African rather than white European descent, I would have had a different set of experiences.

In 2004 I returned to the United States when my husband and I separated. I found myself living in a suburb across a narrow stretch of the Neponset River from Boston's Mattapan neighborhood. Raising a teenaged daughter and finding my way in a country I had left when I was eighteen, I thought little about race beyond seeking out a town and a high school where my daughter would not be the only student of color.

Most of my energy was spent on the uncomfortable and dramatic shift from a Third World to First World perspective, and processing the grief I felt at the ending of my marriage. Eventually, however, I became aware of economic and safety inequities in Boston, with nearby Mattapan and Roxbury experiencing a level of violence and poverty that would not be tolerated in wealthy White neighborhoods in Beacon Hill or the Back Bay. By the time I took a position with The Episcopal Church in 2013, I was glad to be building alliances and programs that focused on addressing racism and social justice. While directing Episcopal Divinity School's Lifelong Learning program, for example, I initiated a pilgrimage that brought people together to revisit civil rights history in order to fuel a present day commitment to dismantling racism.[5]

When asked to write this chapter, I began thinking about local examples where I saw people working together to bring positive change. Among those with whom I spoke was Bithiah Carter, president and founder of New England Blacks in Philanthropy and executive director of the Grand Circle Foundation's Community Advisory Group, a body that works to increase high school and college graduation rates in some of Boston's most economically challenged neighborhoods. Carter and I met in a Cambridge tea shop to talk about her work. As the conversation progressed, she related a recent experience of seeking refinancing for her Boston home. An appraiser came to assess the property, a normal step in the process of ensuring lenders that their loan is in keeping with the value of the property. When Carter received the appraisal value, she was surprised. With a strong financial background and having done her homework, she expected a higher figure. Curious, she decided to conduct an experiment. She put away all family pictures and other items that suggested ties to Africa, and asked her White husband to receive the next appraiser. The new estimate was $130,000 higher, nearly a third of the property's final value.

"And this is not 1960 we're talking about," Carter emphasized. "This is happening today." I did some research to put her anecdote into context, and came across an annual study of home-lending trends. A group led by University of Massachusetts economics professor Jim Campen has identified a persistent racial disparity in mortgage approval rates in the greater Boston area, even when people of color have the same income as Whites. In 2014, Black borrowers had their mortgage applications

---

5 For more information, see my 2014 blog post, "Bridging Past and Present: Reflections on the Jonathan Daniels Pilgrimage," accessed on September 11, 2015, http://eds.edu/news/bridging-past-and-present.

rejected 17 percent of the time; nearly three times the 6 percent rate for White borrowers. The rejection rate for Afro Americans with a salary of $90,000 or more was double that of Euro Americans.[6] An earlier study reviewing Boston's racial gap in mortgage lending confirmed that differences in credit scores and other legitimate measures of borrower risk could only account for half of such disparities; the rest was simply racial discrimination.[7] For Carter this represents "the epicenter of racism" since mortgages and homeownership are crucial assets in people's overall financial health. How, she wondered, do we begin to dismantle this kind of racism?

Carter's next question caught me unprepared. "When you talk about race among White people, what's the tenor of the conversation? How do people talk about it when only White people are around?" I was stumped, finding it hard to picture myself in a strictly White tableau. My circle of relations and friends are diverse, my children are biracial, their father Indian, and during my twenty years of living and working in India, my closest family and work colleagues were all Indians. I tried to explain my feeling of disconnect to Carter, saying I did not know if I had ever been in that kind of conversation with only White people. Why not? she wanted to know. The silence lengthened while I thought about my various experiences. I realized that there usually was someone of color in the group when I had deeper conversations about racism. Carter pressed on: What about when you are just with your White friends—how do you talk about racism then? I pictured sharing coffee or a meal with a small group. Again I was stuck. I explained that when we were together we usually talk about our lives, telling stories, rarely discussing the "isms." Forget deep analysis, Carter pushed. How do you talk about the racism happening all around you: the deaths of unarmed Blacks at the hands of police, the wealth and income gaps? I felt uncomfortable realizing that my deepest discussions about racism were usually in spaces where I knew people shared my passion and beliefs, and those spaces usually included people of color. Listening for an answer that did not come, Carter finally remarked, "Well, maybe that's why we have so little progress. If we can't get even the most well-meaning

6 Jay Fitzgerald, "Black, Latino Mortgage Rejection Rates Still High," *Boston Globe*, December 22, 2015, accessed January 3, 2016, http://www.bostonglobe.com/ business/2015/12/21/blacks-latinos-still-rejected-for-mortgages-higher-rates/ kng3Kuc4v3uIK1pmDqBSjO/story.html?s_campaign=bostonglobe%3Asocialflow% 3Afacebook.

7 Dennis Glennon, and Mitchell Stengel, "An Evaluation of the Federal Reserve Bank of Boston's Study of Racial Discrimination in Mortgage Lending," working paper 94-2 of the Office of the Comptroller of the Currency, Economic and Policy Analysis, 1994.

White people to think about racism when they don't have to, I guess racism will never change."

I felt shame in the face of Carter's challenge. Her questions not only forced me to use Whiteness as a frame for my social interactions, it pushed me to think about where and when I addressed racism. Although in some ways my life could be seen as a story about crossing boundaries of race and privilege, her pointed questions suggested ways I still might be holding back. As I reflected, I realized that the stories I felt most drawn to tell about dismantling racism were those led solely or collaboratively by people of color. I valued spaces where people worked hard to come together across barriers like race and class. What about the responsibility Whites like me have for working within our own communities to dismantle systemic oppressions? Could the injustice of Carter's refinancing experience ever change if we did not leverage our power and privilege to engage other White people? And how might that engagement be most transformative?

Reflecting on these questions and processing this uncomfortable encounter strengthened my commitment to work more intentionally in White spaces. I'm grateful to Bithiah Carter for risking honest engagement, and helping me to grow by challenging my ideas. I have new energy and curiosity for designing creative, encouraging, and transformative processes that help galvanize White people to reconciliation and action. I also am inspired by local groups who are engaged deeply in this work, including Community Change, Inc., a Boston-based non-profit that has been addressing the roots of racism in White communities for almost fifty years; and White People Challenging Racism: Moving from Talk to Action, a grassroots initiative that for more than fifteen years has been helping White people gain tools to challenge and change attitudes and actions that perpetuate racism. I am excited by the national network Showing Up for Racial Justice (SURJ) that since 2009 has been motivating, training, and connecting White individuals and groups in an effort to build a strong movement of collective action.

It is not those stories, though, that I wish to tell. I focus in the rest of the chapter on initiatives led by people of color, or Blacks and Whites together. These are local stories of people working to dismantle racism: a community health center that identifies how racism impacts health and decides to do something about it; community organizers who discover a collective trauma inhibiting people's public engagement and devise a process to revisit and learn from that painful history; and an initiative catalyzed by business leaders that helps students gain new connections to and energy from the American civil rights journey. I have chosen to focus on efforts taking place in the greater Boston area not because this city is a leader in dismantling racism and building Beloved Community, but to encourage readers to explore your own towns, cities, and states to discover the courageous, transformative often unheralded work going on there.

Mobilizing around Structural Racism

The Southern Jamaica Plain Health Center (SJPHC) designed a model of racial reconciliation and healing that connects health to the empowerment of communities around social and racial justice. Like most community health centers, this one has a mission to improve health and well-being by educating community members about ways to preserve and promote health. SJPHC is part of a Boston network of twenty-five health centers reaching underserved communities, and offers primary care to 12,000 racially and economically diverse residents of Jamaica Plain and surrounding neighborhoods. The choice to focus on racial reconciliation sprang from Executive Director Tom Kieffer and others realizing that people's sickness or wellness are less a product of their lifestyle choices than larger societal factors. The Health Center staff decided to address these head-on.

Data from Boston shows persistent racial inequity in health outcomes and mortality rates.[8] The most dramatic example of this is a 33-year gap in life expectancy between people living in an affluent White Back Bay neighborhood between Massachusetts Avenue and Arlington Street (91.9 years), and those living in a similar-sized Roxbury neighborhood demarcated by Dudley Street, Shawmut Avenue, Massachusetts Avenue, and Albany Street (58.9 years). Infant mortality in the city is twice as high for Black babies as it is for White ones, and hospitalizations of young children with asthma is three times higher among Blacks than Whites. The Boston Public Health Commission's annual *Health of Boston Report* regularly chronicles a long list of other appalling health inequities.[9]

Data shows that racial disparities of this magnitude are not caused by lack of access to health care. Health and longevity are affected most

---

8   Emily Zimmerman, Benjamin F. Evans, Steven H. Woolf, and Amber D. Haley, *Social Capital and Health Outcomes in Boston* (Richmond: Center on Human Needs, Virginia Commonwealth University, 2012), accessed September 15, 2015, http://www.societyhealth.vcu.edu/media/society-health/pdf/PMReport_Boston.pdf.

9   Available on the Boston Public Health Commission website: www.bphc.org/healthdata/health-of-boston-report/Pages/Health-of-Boston-Report.aspx.

powerfully by factors such as safe, affordable housing; job opportunities; socioeconomic status; education; environmental exposure; access to fresh, healthy food; and so on. These social determinants of health are, in turn, heavily influenced by deep, structural racism. For example, unfair mortgage practices and unequal job opportunities make it more difficult for people of color to own homes, while red-lining and other more subtle discriminatory practices have limited financial resources and other services in neighborhoods of low-income residents or people of color. In addition, segregated, poorer localities like Roxbury and Mattapan contain a disproportionate number of direct health risks, including environmental hazard sites, polluting industries, and waste processing centers. On the flip side they offer only limited access to health-enhancing resources, whether safe places to play and exercise, high quality child care, excellent schools, or grocery stores supplying fresh, healthy food. Data shows that such indirect "upstream" factors have the greatest impact on people's long-term health.[10]

Aware of these facts and supported by a shift in understanding at the Boston Public Health Commission level,[11] Kieffer and his staff decided not only to put resources into "downstream" interventions like education programs for Black men threatened with diabetes, but also to educate and mobilize the community about the institutionalized racism that increases Black men's risk for diabetes; for example, food access, and inequitable housing and employment policies. The focus thus has shifted from palliative treatment to illness prevention; from health disparities to health inequities. Staff now help residents understand the systemic roots of racial differences in sickness and wellness, and support and encourage them to collaborate on efforts to bring change.

The Health Center chose to put special effort into educating and mentoring young people on this issue. Abigail Ortiz, the director of Community Health programs, and Dennie Butler-MacKay, a clinically licensed social worker with specialties in trauma, adolescence, and racism, started the Racial Reconciliation and Healing project in 2010. The yearlong program unites White youth and youth of color with the explicit goal of dismantling racism in all areas where social structures

---

10 For a compelling explanation of this, see the seven-part documentary film series, "Unnatural Causes: Is Inequality Making Us Sick?": http://www.unnaturalcauses.org/.

11 Nashira Baril et al., "Building a Regional Health Equity Movement: The Grantmaking Model of a Local Health Department," *Family & Community Health* 34, supplement 1S (2011): S23–S43, accessed December 10, 2015, www.bphc.org/whatwedo/health-equity-social-justice/racial-justice-health-equity-initiative/Documents/BuildingaRegionalHealthEquityMovement.pdf.

impact people's health. Each year the Center recruits and awards a modest stipend to sixteen students between the ages of sixteen and twenty-two, bringing them together twice weekly to create an intentional space for processing the enormously painful data around what is making people sick. Ortiz and Butler-MacKay encourage students to stay for multiple years if possible.[12]

Each "racial rec" cohort is half White and half students of color and mirrors the inequities of life in Boston. Young people of color largely come from low-income families and attend poorly resourced public schools. Ortiz notes that most have a heightened awareness about racism but lack the language or analysis to talk about it. White students generally attend better ranked schools and have access to greater opportunities. These and other differences are integrated into the process, underscoring the fact that people of color and Whites come at racism—and the work of dismantling it—from different perspectives. Latino and Afro American youth begin with an initial healing process, while White students start with a focus on reconciliation.

Ortiz and Butler-MacKay stress that racism has traumatized people of all races, and encourage participants to recognize and deal with emotions that come up while engaging it. They see the program as more than an academic exercise. Uniting head and heart is essential if people are to sustain a long-term commitment to addressing and dismantling systemic racism. Readings, racial affinity groups, workshops, healing circles, speak-outs, and fieldwork all help young people deal with issues head-on and explore pathways to change. In the process, young men and women learn how to better express themselves and interact safely with people from different racial or class groups. Students who stay for a second year design a fieldwork project, directly applying what they have learned.

One of the most challenging areas in this work is recognizing the different roles White people and people of color play. Many Whites tend to see racial justice work as led by people of color. Looking to the civil rights era, we see African Americans defining the problem, shaping strategies, and leading the movement. White people yielded leadership and expressed solidarity by showing up at rallies, marches, and sit-ins; doing whatever was necessary to support the struggle. For many White activists, grassroots organizing provided a clear frame for engagement: work in solidarity with people who have been oppressed, respect their strength and leadership, and do not seek to dominate the space or decide

---

12 Personal communication, May 15, 2015.

for others what can or should be done. Over the years we have deputized people of color to be our diversity officers, having them take on the role of educating White people and holding them accountable on issues of racial oppression and justice.

But now, says Ortiz, "it's racism 2.0." Racism is so deeply ingrained in our social policies and practices that we can perpetuate it unknowingly in environments that are race silent. In such a climate we no longer can afford the illusion that this is a problem only for people of color. We are very clear, says Ortiz. If racism is an exploitive system set up by White people, maintained by White people, and benefiting White people, who has the primary responsibility for dismantling it? Although Euro Americans may stand in solidarity with the Black Lives Matter movement, for example, their primary role is in White spaces where no one is talking about race. This might be a workplace where all the employees are White and the company is planning to buy a building that will displace local residents of color in a gentrifying neighborhood. Or it might be a procurement meeting where once again all the businesses the company chooses to work with are White owned. Or a neighborhood school where White teachers and administrators explain away a persistent achievement gap between Black and White students.

It can be uncomfortable to speak up about equity and diversity, advocating in White spaces for a different reality. It can be risky to be known as the person who always raises awkward questions. Yet this is work crucial to the spiritual well-being of *all* people; it is not work Whites do on behalf of Afro Americans or Latinos or others. It is only by taking ownership of dismantling racist systems and overcoming our own racial assumptions that we can create the just, loving, compassionate world for which we long.

White leadership on the frontlines of dismantling racism is important for another reason: people of color need to do their own work. "If Whites took down the structures of White supremacy tomorrow and people of color have not done their own healing work," says Butler-MacKay, "the impact of racism would not end." Helping oneself and one's community heal from internalized oppression is especially challenging because we tend to overlook the value of this kind of work. Healing gained through protest and struggle is more readily acknowledged and valued. To make progress in this area and create lasting change, we need the most talented people of color working within their own communities. The painful conversations about internalized racial oppression need to take place among people of color. They are not White conversations. If working to educate

White people or dismantle racism in White spaces takes all the attention and energy of leaders of color, we have depleted a crucial resource for bringing healing and change to our society.

The chief outcome of the Racial Reconciliation and Healing program has been to grow the number of people able to talk about racism and to initiate efforts to transform it. The program has created ties among an activated and empowered multiracial group committed to racial equity.[13] Some of the fruit is already being seen in initiatives begun by former participants, including the Get Health Information Project (GetHIP) that encourages young men of color to be advocates for health equity, designing media campaigns about specific issues from oral health to incarceration.[14]

The Southern Jamaica Plain Health Center's initiative is a concrete and powerful form of reconciliation and healing work. Part of its power lies in bringing the painful truth of systemic racism to the center of community awareness, and supporting people to envision and create change. It offers a space where people confront racism head-on and talk through the anger, guilt, and other emotions arising from the harsh reality of health inequities. Participants not only learn skills that help them advocate for racial justice at key structural levels, they also deepen a commitment to engage, challenge, and support each other in doing this work together.

Revisiting Uncomfortable Parts of Our History

As a newcomer to Boston in 2004, I rarely heard about the court-ordered desegregation of Boston's schools mandated in 1974. When I did, it was referred to as "the busing crisis." White friends explained it as a crazy and violent time when community was pitted against community. I was confused about what really happened but never heard enough of the story to get a full picture. It is a period many Bostonians prefer to put behind them. Sal LaMattina, a member of the Boston City Council and an employee of the city since 1989, recently confessed, "As a White politician, I was always told we don't talk about busing. We are a better city

---

13 For a powerful introduction to this program, see the 2012 documentary produced by Intercultural Productions in collaboration with SJPHC, the Boston Public Health Commission, and the Kellogg Foundation: www.youtube.com/watch?v=84imro3UVig.

14 For more information about the Racial Reconciliation and Healing program, see the page on Racial Justice and Health Equity Work on the website of Brigham and Women's Hospital (the licensing body for SJPHC): www.brighamandwomens.org/Departments_and_ Services/medicine/services/primarycare/sjphc/RacialJustice_and_healthequity. aspx?sub=0.

than we were forty years ago."[15] Yet it is this very history that community organizers stumbled over when trying to mobilize people to improve Boston's public schools. The Union of Minority Neighborhoods eventually realized that in order to create positive change in the present, Boston residents would need to speak about and learn from an ugly and traumatic part of their past.

According to the 2010 census, roughly 53 percent of Boston citizens identify as something other than non-Hispanic White, making this state capital a "minority majority" city. The student body attending Boston public schools is among the most racially and ethnically diverse in the nation—87 percent are students of color, and nearly one in two speaks a language other than English at home. Race and zip code are closely intertwined, however. When combined with neighboring Cambridge and Newton, the Boston area becomes the seventh most highly segregated metropolitan region in the nation, somewhat less segregated than Nashville but more than Birmingham.[16] Not surprisingly, this segregation reflects economic and educational disparities as well. Forty-two percent of children living in the core neighborhoods of color—Roxbury, Dorchester, and Mattapan—are economically disadvantaged, the largest concentration of child poverty in the state. This is also where ten of Boston's twelve chronically "underperforming" schools are located. Inequitable access to resources, low expectations for success, and the criminalization of school discipline are among a host of factors contributing to a stubborn achievement gap along the fault lines of race and economic security. The largest casualty are Black boys who currently test out to be half as proficient in English and math as White ones.[17]

Many people have suggested that fixing race and class inequities in Boston's schools requires the involvement of local families and communities. For the Union of Minority Neighborhoods (UMN), this strategy is primary. Founded in 2002 by community organizer and activist Horace Small, the UMN aims to unify and train people of color to successfully address neighborhood, regional, and national problems. Early in 2010

15 Yawu Miller, "Busing Forum Bridges Decades-Old Divide," *The Bay State Banner*, online edition, June 25, 2014, accessed September 11, 2015, http://baystatebanner.com/news/2014/jun/25/busing-forum-bridges-decades-old-divide/?page=1.

16 Alexander Kent and Thomas C. Frohlich, "America's Most Segregated Cities," accessed October 23, 2015, http://247wallst.com/special-report/2015/08/19/americas-most-segregated-cities/2/.

17 Boston Public Schools, "Every Student, Every Day: Eliminating Achievement and Opportunity Gaps," last modified November 5, 2014, accessed October 24, 2015: www.bostonpublicschools.org/cms/lib07/MA01906464/Centricity/Domain/162/AchievementGap11052014.pdf.

they initiated Black People for Better Public Schools, bringing together parents, residents, and others invested in local neighborhoods to share their perceptions of public schools and their ideas for how to improve them. After quite a few such town hall meetings, the leadership team identified a pattern in the community's deep cynicism and distrust of the school system. People's experiences of school desegregation in the 1970s had left a legacy of pain, including a residue of unprocessed anger and grief. Individuals and whole communities had experienced trauma and loss. So many students from this period had dropped out or received a shaky education that their cohort was sometimes referred to as "the lost generation." The UMN team concluded that any movement to imagine and create a new future for Boston schools required revisiting and processing that traumatic time together.

UMN began by asking a small group of leaders with strong ties to local communities whether they thought such an endeavor worthwhile. The answer was a conditional "yes": it had value as long as it helped address contemporary challenges. Encouraged, the UMN team launched an active neighborhood listening process to find out how the era had touched Asian, Afro and Euro American, and Latino communities. The stories revealed important differences in language: in White circles people talked about the "busing" crisis, while Black folks usually spoke about "desegregation"—busing was simply about transportation. Honoring these differences, UMN called their initiative the Boston Busing/Desegregation Project (BBDP), and stressed their commitment to learning from the stories, lessons, and questions of people whose lives were directly impacted by this tumultuous period.

By June 2011, BBDP had reached out to potential collaborators and funders and enlisted media producer Scott Mercer to capture some of people's stories in a short documentary film. Project Director Donna Bivens and a small staff and team of volunteers then partnered with dozens of community based groups across the city to screen *Can We Talk? Learning from Boston's Busing/Desegregation Crisis*. At each viewing they asked the audience what about this history was relevant for today. The listening exercise surfaced three themes that were important during and leading up to the 1970s watershed period and continue to have relevance today: racial and class equity, democratic access to resources and decision making, and demanding excellence of public institutions.

BBDP committed itself to building leadership that could find contemporary meaning in these themes and work to collectively address them. They pulled together a Learning Network to guide and support a process of community truth-telling. This diverse and evolving group of men and women brought together wide-ranging knowledge and skills to help learn from and refine the truth-telling process and to support communities through it. The team hoped that deep, respectful listening to people's stories in community would bear witness to individual and collective wounds and hopes, and would help people move beyond old misunderstandings to see and embrace successes and shared values. Bivens and her colleagues also hoped that it would energize a cadre of leaders to transform Boston into a city that honors the need to speak honestly about the realities of the color divide and concentrated wealth, and works together to transform these barriers.

BBDP began to convene "story circles," an artistic and community-building technique that rests on the premise that everyone has a story to tell, and that externalizing one's story, constructing a narrative, and through it reconstructing history, is therapeutic.[18] Emerson College professor Robbie McCauley trained facilitators in the process, and BBDP began holding circles throughout the city so that people could speak about their relationship to busing/desegregation history. Acknowledging that there are many aspects of truth about what happened during this era, leaders encouraged people not to judge others' experiences but to share their own: What do you remember? How do you understand and connect to this history? How has that history affected you today? What can we learn from it? A choice was made to convene racial affinity groups so people could better hear and understand their story within a single race context. It soon became clear that this was complicated by class, culture, and ethnicity, with leaders learning that there are many stories outside the simple context of "Black" or "White." A later phase united people across race to talk about their shared history. By the end of 2014, more than 3,000 people had participated in story circles and other BBDP forums.

The process highlighted that there are at least two separate narratives about this history. The dominant one, voiced by the majority of Whites living in Boston, framed the story in terms of a 1974 court order mandating children be bused between predominantly White and Black neighborhoods. For over two years violent racial protests and rioting pitted

18 John O'Neal and his colleagues at Junebug Productions in New Orleans developed story circles as a way to create oral history of African American experience. For more about this technique, see the 2006 unpublished report by New York University's Research Center for Leadership in Action Leadership for a Changing World, "Using Art and Theater to Support Organizing for Justice," accessed January 8, 2016, http://www.racialequitytools.org/resourcefiles/nyuwagner.pdf.

working class communities in South Boston, Charlestown, and Roxbury against each other. Protesting parents, students, and others hurled rocks, bottles, and racial epithets at buses of students, and demonstrations and sit-outs led schools to close for days at a time. The State Police and the National Guard became a visible presence on local streets and in schools, and for well over a decade control of the desegregation plan remained with the courts. The turmoil accelerated the flight of the White middle class from the city to the suburbs, and 30,000 mostly White students left Boston public schools for suburban, parochial, and private ones. The era was traumatizing for Whites as well as Blacks. As Georgianna Johnson, a South Boston resident described, "We had children who witnessed adults at their ugliest, who were pulled out of school, who learned only to have contempt for education and authority, and who then gave birth to their own children."[19]

The second narrative, framed by Afro Americans, located the tumultuous events of the 1970s within a long justice struggle around the distribution of public resources. The first time the Boston School Committee's efforts to racially segregate schools had been contested was in 1849 when Benjamin F. Roberts challenged the requirement that his five-year-old daughter Sarah enroll in an all-Black public school. She and other Afro American children had to walk past five neighborhood elementary schools in Beacon Hill before reaching the poor and densely crowded Abiel Smith School. Eventually the Massachusetts Supreme Court ruled against Roberts, arguing that "separate but equal" facilities were legal, a principle that became popular in advancing educational segregation across the nation until it was invalidated by the Supreme Court in the 1954 Brown v. the Board of Education ruling. Yet even after Roberts lost his case, Boston's free Black community continued to agitate against denying children the right to attend neighborhood schools. The community engaged in boycotts, protests, the strategic use of White allies, and the creation of new outlets for their message. Within five years they had pushed Boston to become the first major city in the United States to open public schools to children of African descent.[20]

---

19 Georgianna Johnson, "There Was Much City Could, and Should, Have Done before Garrity's Ruling," letter to the editor, *Boston Globe*, June 28, 2014; downloaded November 24, 2015, from www.bostonglobe.com/opinion/editorials/2014/06/27/there-was-much-city-could-and-should-have-done-before-garrity-ruling/3EptUymHQhhR34obwQX4ZJ/story.html.

20 More about this history can be found in Stephen and Paul Kendrick's wonderful book *Sarah's Long Walk: The Free Blacks of Boston and How Their Struggle for Equality Changed America* (Boston: Beacon Press, 2004).

This win did not resolve racism in the schools, however. Unequal educational opportunity and ongoing racial discrimination catalyzed protests in the 1960s, culminating in the state's 1965 Racial Imbalance Act requiring schools to desegregate if their student body was more than 50 percent of one race. Boston's School Committee, whose five elected members were all White, refused to comply, arguing that the racial profiles of schools reflected population demographics not intentional segregation, and that all school children had equal resources and opportunities. Black parents protested, boycotting city schools, organizing separate "freedom schools," and arranging buses and carpools to take their children from neighborhood schools to suburban White ones. In 1972 with the help of the National Association for the Advancement of Colored People, fourteen Black parents and their children filed a class action lawsuit against the Boston Public School Committee. The court ruled in favor of the parents and children after reviewing evidence that the School Committee unequally allocated materials and resources, kept schools racially segregated by gerrymandering neighborhood boundaries, and discriminated along the lines of race in hiring, assigning, and promoting faculty and staff.

Thus, for Black residents of Boston, the events of the 1970s did not occur in isolation. Framing this era as a crisis over busing evokes an imagined harmonious past that was disrupted only by a divisive court order. Such a portrayal not only minimizes a complex history stretching for centuries, it also fails to examine the power dynamics that have kept systems of oppression in place. BBDP leaders hope that creating and learning from a shared story will energize people to question the stories they had inherited, and ultimately shift the underlying, repeating pattern of the use of power to benefit some individuals and communities while excluding and oppressing others.

- After more than four years of listening and learning, Bivens and her team are clear that reconciliation from the trauma and wounds of this period has barely begun. Lessons carved out in community have surfaced a number of questions including:

  » Whose story is it and how do we navigate the power differences that allow a master narrative to continue to reassert itself and drown out more marginalized stories?

  » Whose city is it when longtime residents and communities are displaced by "luxury" condos and cookie-cutter high rises?

> » Is [the issue] about racism or is it about class and how
> do we attain the race and class literacy that can help us
> escape that either/or choice?

> » What is excellence [for example, in our public schools]
> when access to it is such a function of privilege?[21]

BBDP is currently focused on a public-learning campaign that takes questions like these back to local community-based partners. The aim is to work collaboratively on creating "race and class literacy" through neighborhood workshops and the development and distribution of educational materials. Change will come, says Bivens, as people better understand how race and class shape their everyday lives, including through decision making at governing levels in Boston, the state, and the country. BBDP is strengthening a core group of people of all races who can address such issues and together create new solutions to problems like the ones plaguing Boston's public schools.

Indeed, one of the tangible fruits of BBDP's work has been inspiring and supporting the rewrite of the desegregation curriculum of Boston Public Schools (BPS). For years when history and social studies teachers taught about race relations, discrimination, and the work of desegregation, they drew on examples from Arkansas and other southern states. In 2015 BPS leaders reached out to Donna Bivens and a team of colleagues, including Jose Lopez and Paula Elliott, to help devise a new curriculum. Together with other organizations and individuals, they assembled resources to help students better understand what happened in Boston, from the red-lining of neighborhoods, to segregated housing, to the violent struggle to desegregate schools. The new curriculum not only helps students learn about a history that affected their neighbors and family members, it helps them become more aware of patterns of structural racism and class privilege that continue today.

The power of the Boston Busing/Desegregation Project lies in naming and engaging a traumatic and painful part of our past that continues to influence our present. Traditionally, the making of history has been a process of selecting which stories to tell and which to leave out. In contrast, BBDP has committed to convening spaces where every story has a

---

21 From UMN's December 18, 2014, blog post "BBDP Year-End Update & Request," accessed December 20, 2015, http://bbdproject.org/2014/12/18/bbdp-year-end-update-request/. BBDP's work has been distilled in several reports available on its website http://bbdproject. org/, including the 2014 "Unfinished Business: Linking Boston's 'Busing/Desegregation Crisis' to Struggles for Equity, Access and Excellence for All in Boston Today" that highlights seven key learnings from the work. Accessed on October 23, 2015, from https:// bbdplearningnetwork.files.wordpress.com/2014/09/7-lessons-bbdp-9-11-14.pdf.

chance to be heard, valued, and mined for the lessons it offers. Leaders realized that the process of creating a narrative is of equal or greater importance than the narrative itself. It is the process of listening, discovering, and learning together that helps to mitigate lingering trauma and to empower people to begin creating a new story together.

Energizing Deeper Engagement

Our final example of dismantling racism began with a "What if . . . ?" question at a 2014 dinner party in New York City. Prominent Afro American business leaders and philanthropists had come together for an intimate New Year's Eve celebration among friends. A few among the group had attended early screenings of the movie *Selma* and talk around the table was enthusiastic and energized. Eventually someone wondered what might happen if every child in America—Black and White—could see this powerful portrayal of a defining moment in our history. How might it nurture, strengthen, and inspire young people, creating even more energy for change? These simple wonderings set in motion an unprecedented campaign that underwrote the costs for 300,000 students to see the movie in theatres across the country, and culminated in every high school in the nation receiving a DVD copy of the film and a curriculum guide with suggested ways to use it.

Selma chronicles the dangerous American civil rights campaign to secure equal voting rights in the face of violent opposition. Part of the film's power lies in offering a glimpse into the organized yet fractious movement that was the driving force behind the passage of the 1965 Voting Rights Act. Set during a tumultuous three-month period that culminates in the 1965 march from Selma to Montgomery, it brings to life the complicated, brilliant, flawed man who was Martin Luther King Jr. and accurately shows the civil rights movement as shaped by women and young people as well as men. It also captures the tensions between key groups, including King's Southern Christian Leadership Conference and the young activists of the Student Nonviolent Coordinating Committee. Director Ava DuVernay and her racially diverse and highly talented cast and crew not only offer viewers a window into the sacrifices, victories, and losses behind a defining moment in US history, they also illuminate the complex and nuanced story of how real change takes place.

The film struck a powerful chord with the group gathered in New York City that New Year's Eve. It came at a time when the killing of unarmed black men including Trayvon Martin, Michael Brown, Tamir

Rice, and Eric Garner had elicited a feeling of hopeless frustration within the Black community. Anyone with a Black son—whether they worked in a gas station or were CEO of a major corporation—knew this could happen to their child. It was always part of dinner and cocktail party conversation, observed Bennie Wiley, former president and CEO of The Partnership, Inc., a Boston-based organization that supports multicultural professionals and helps corporations and institutions attract, develop, and retain talented leaders of color. People did not know what to do beyond expressing concern, frustration, and fear for their own children. The movie not only provided a sense of historical context for current struggles, it also brought to life the courage and determination of a generation of men and women on whose shoulders everyone stood. It helped leaders like those gathered in New York City to see more clearly the arc of their own journey.

Bennie Wiley and her husband, Fletcher "Flash" Wiley, were the only Bostonites present that evening. All others were New York City–based social and business powerhouses, including Bill Lewis and wife, Carol Sutton Lewis; Kenneth and Kathryn Chenault; Tony and Robyn Coles; and Charles and Karen Phillips. The group began to discuss ways that young people might have a chance to see the movie. Charles Phillips, a member of the Board of Viacom, offered to reach out to the leadership there to get in touch with Paramount Pictures, one of its subsidiaries and the distributor for the movie. Perhaps if they could raise the money for tickets, Paramount might streamline students' access to them. All agreed to commit themselves financially and try to get the project moving quickly since *Selma* was scheduled to open widely in theaters in just over a week.

When she returned to Boston, Wiley didn't give the proposal too much thought, expecting it to be just one more good idea raised over cocktails. A week later one of her friends called from New York to share news of the unbelievable response they had received and to encourage Wiley to mobilize in Boston. Reaching out to friends and acquaintances, the New York circle had raised $280,000 in a matter of days. Paramount Pictures agreed to let its network of theaters honor any student who showed a valid ID or report card, and offered to charge benefactors a special rate of $10 for each student ticket. Now the group was spreading the word to everyone with a connection to seventh, eighth, and ninth grade students, from the New York Public Library to the Harlem Children's Zone, the Apollo Theater to the Abyssinian Baptist Church. The Mayor's Office and the Department of Education announced their support, and by the time the campaign was over, more than two dozen Afro American business and community leaders had enabled 75,000 New York City–area school students to see *Selma* the first weekend of its wide theatrical release.

Wiley knew the Black community in Boston did not have the same wealth as the one in New York, but she figured there was nothing to lose in trying a similar effort in her city. Setting a goal of $100,000, she started going through her rolodex contacting prominent leaders who might make sizeable contributions. She deliberately chose to focus on the Afro American community, forgoing White, corporate, or foundation support. She knew that having the Black community extend their own resources to sponsor children of all races to see this film was itself a strong, empowering message. The Boston Foundation, where she is a longtime board member, made available a tax-deductible account to receive donations for the project. People's immediate and enthusiastic responses were exhilarating and within five days the campaign had raised $120,000.

By then Wiley had shifted her energy to seeing that children took advantage of the sponsored tickets. Since the movie had already opened, the target became getting middle and high school students into theaters over the long Martin Luther King Jr. weekend. Everyone who contributed was asked to spread the word, while Wiley and other volunteers reached out to Black political figures, the Black ministerial community, and school and nonprofit leaders, urging them to pass the information on to their constituencies. Boston Public Schools and local charter schools sent word out to teachers, parents, and students, and the Boston Foundation informed their large network of nonprofits. Teachers, youth workers, and church leaders began organizing field trips, and many parents and relatives took their children on their own. When the campaign finally ran its course, nearly 11,000 students in the Boston metropolitan area had seen the film.

The wave continued beyond Boston. Bennie Wiley joined New York initiators in contacting friends across the country, urging them to coordinate similar efforts in their own communities. The group began a website and social media campaign, inviting students and teachers who made use of the opportunity to share their reflections using the hashtag "#SelmaforStudents." By the end of February, 2.5 million dollars had been raised and 300,000 students in thirty-three cities and regions had attended local theaters. These results were unprecedented: never before had business leaders coordinated and underwritten such a massive national campaign to enable people to view a film with an important message. But the group continued to dream bigger. What if every student in the nation had the opportunity to see the film? What if teachers and other leaders could draw on strong resource materials to help young people process what they saw? With the invigorating support of this community of changemakers, Paramount announced in April 2015 that it would send a DVD of the movie to every US high school free of charge. In addition, an extensive curriculum guide offering interdisciplinary lesson plans in history, English language arts, mathematics, art, and geography was made available through BazanED, an online source for free multicultural teaching materials.

The power of this initiative lies in people recognizing that a film like *Selma* creates opportunities for real conversation about issues that collectively feed, divide, trouble, and traumatize us. For many people in the Euro American community, there is a deep discomfort talking about racism. Yet if we want to develop strategies and solutions that can dismantle it, we need open, candid talk among everyone who is part of the system. Racism is so deeply ingrained in American culture that there is little chance it will dissipate quickly. But long-term change is built in part through spaces uniting media that powerfully engages our emotions with conversation that inspires us to honesty and vulnerability. The Selma for Students initiative has increased the number of such spaces.

Ingredients for Creating Change

The above practical examples of dismantling racism involve a few common elements. The biggest is the creation of space where people can have conversations neither simple nor superficial about racism. These occasions may take the shape of truth-telling about a painful part of our history or our present, debriefing a film that stirred our emotions, or some other form. They may occur through facilitated meetings, in classrooms, or among small groups of friends, neighbors, or parishioners. Wherever and however they happen, they are sacred spaces. They are sacred because countless men and women, children and the elderly have lost their lives and continue to lose them through the evil of racism. They also are sacred because they touch a place where our spirits have been wounded and where our brokenness makes us vulnerable. This is not true only for people of color; it is true for Whites as well. My own brokenness becomes visible when a person's skin color elicits my response and diminishes my connection to a unique human being. My spirit is wounded by being a part of a church, community, and nation that all have gained wealth and security through the unacknowledged exploitation of people of color. Finally, these spaces are sacred because when people intentionally come together for real and difficult conversations, they bring with them the seeds for transformation and new life.

A second common element, indivisible from such spaces, is deep listening. People take a risk when they choose to tell their stories or share painful emotions with others. Taking such a risk is an act of intentional and heroic vulnerability. Our response helps to create or diminish a climate of trust between the speaker and his or her listeners. White people like myself have much to learn about sacred listening in racially diverse spaces. In his honest and impassioned 2015 sermon at Bethel United Church of Christ in White Salmon, Washington, Afro American writer John Metta admitted that he has spent a lifetime not talking to White people about racism. His choice is based on experience, for whenever he has tried, even with beloved family members, the conversation quickly shifted to the White person seeking to prove that they themselves were not racist or arguing that racism does not exist because they had never experienced it.[22]

Metta suggests that in the United States we do not talk easily about racism because we are part of a society that prioritizes the feelings of White people over the lives of Black people. Our focus on taking care of White people, on safeguarding the feelings of those of us who do not want to see ourselves as racist keeps us from engaging, understanding, and dismantling the racist systems we help to sustain. Denial and defensiveness shut down dialogue and inhibit trust. White people like myself need to take responsibility for listening well and for processing any hurt that we feel in response to the testimony of people of color. We need to unpack our defensiveness, coming to grips with whatever shame, anger, fear, or guilt we uncover. This is perhaps most effectively done in affinity groups. Doing such work in spaces where people come together across race can take time and energy away from learning how to think about and dismantle the systemic racism our Whiteness gives us the privilege not to see.

A third common element to all three accounts of dismantling racism is that the leaders of each initiative leveraged their own unique power to fuel change. The success of the Selma for Students campaign, for example, is tied to the gifts and resources business leaders brought to

---

22 Published online July 6, 2015, as "I, Racist" in the magazine *Those People*. Accessed on January 5, 2015, from https://thsppl.com/i-racist-538512462265#.cn36ee9py.

the task, including a network of contacts, strong organizing and promotion skills, access to capital and key decision makers, and their influence as men and women whose opinions others respect. Leaders at the Southern Jamaica Plain Health Center inspired and trained residents to confront the structural racism behind health inequities by leveraging the power associated with being part of Boston's health network, including a dedicated staff, community connections, and awareness of funding sources. The Union of Minority Neighborhoods continues to expand a climate in which all Boston children have the opportunity to flourish by leveraging deep community networks, a commitment to respecting the stories of each individual and group, and skills in creating transformative processes where people can speak and hear each other. Dismantling racism needs more than vision, inspiration, and a thirst for justice. It also requires us to recognize and mobilize the power we have to catalyze change.

I began this chapter by offering a window into my own journey of recovering from racism. There is an inherent messiness to this work, for we are learning still how to do it well. In our attempts to recover from racism, we cannot avoid tripping over unexamined assumptions, biases, pain, and hurt. Changing the very soup in which we swim is no easy task and will take the work of many generations. We will feel uncomfortable at best, enraged, saddened, despondent, and despairing at worst. Can we compassionately accept that this is part of the process as we strive to create Beloved Community? Can we value honesty, courage, and compassion as we hold each other accountable and celebrate our achievements? Can we keep returning to spaces where we try, fail, and rise again so that together we can explore what brought us to our present circumstance and build pathways to a different future?

Catherine Meeks reminded us earlier that recovering from racism is a spiritual discipline and part of our individual and collective journey toward wholeness. One of the tools that has given me strength along the way is one of the baptismal promises made by Episcopalians. In my worshipping community we regularly affirm five vows.[23] These are uplifting reminders for me of our collective and individual spiritual quest. In one, for example, we promise, "to strive for justice and peace among all people and respect the dignity of every human being." The vow that has been particularly life-giving in my work of recovering from racism is to "persevere in resisting evil, and, whenever [I] fall into sin, repent and return

---

23 The full Baptismal Covenant can be found in the Book of Common Prayer (New York: Church Publishing, 1979), beginning on page 304.

to the Lord." This promise reminds me that I will fall into sin, including tripping on racism that exists within and around me. There is no "if" in the vow. But it also offers me two clear steps to take when this happens: to see my mistake and choose to change, and to reclaim my place in the mysterious and all-encompassing love and compassion of God. This love and compassion is often expressed most powerfully through Beloved Community. The stories of the Racial Reconciliation and Healing program, the Boston Busing/Desegregation Project, and the Selma for Students campaign are all efforts worth celebrating, supporting, lifting up, and learning from. There are thousands of others across the country and around our world. Each represents an individual or collective choice or action, perhaps like a point of light in a vast expanse of stars. Maybe that's the secret of transforming our soup. As we step back, we can see the beauty of the light amidst the darkness, and know that as one star goes out, others are born in our ever-evolving journey toward wholeness.

7 Architects of Safe Space for Beloved Community

Lynn W. Huber

The title of this chapter comes from an encounter I had with a young woman who had come to me for spiritual direction, and who began by asking what a spiritual director is. One of the metaphors which occurred to me is that a spiritual director is an architect of safe space. In that space we can explore our inner world, allowing the Holy One to enter it and to lead us, step by step, where we need to go.

One of the places I believe we are called to go *collectively*, especially in our houses of prayer, is toward the goal of Beloved Community. Too often, churches in this country have not promoted the kind of Beloved Community that reflects and celebrates the diversity of our nation, nor have many of them worked toward it. In fact, it appears to me that at many times they have worked actively against it.

In this chapter we are going to address the importance and power of story. Story is a major way of establishing connections between and among events and creating meaning from them. It is the way the elders pass on our history. It is the way our philosophy and our values take on life for us. It is powerful in creating community, and equally capable of creating enemies.

We will also consider ways we can create safe space, individually and collectively, to let God in, to look honestly at ourselves (both our gifts and our challenges and wounds), trusting that if we do this with a willing heart and an open mind, we will be directed to the creation of Beloved

Community that invites all of God's children. The need for this safe space includes the recognition that for each of us, this work demands a two-directional focus, on the one hand, moving into the inner work that heals wounds, opens eyes, and *en-courages* us, and on the other hand, being drawn out into the external world, both to learn and to work.

Let us turn first to story.

The Power of Story

I have believed in the importance of story at least since I was a young sociology major in college.

I once found a statement about story in a book by Jean Shinoda Bolen that ties it clearly to our goal of creating the Beloved Community. It has helped me appreciate the fact that meaning is in the narrative about events, not in the events themselves.

> To bring about a paradigm shift in the culture that will change assumptions and attitudes, a critical number of us have to tell the stories of our personal revelations and transformations. . . . The stories people tell have a way of taking care of them. If stories come to you, care for them. And learn to give them away where they are needed. Sometimes a person needs a story more than food to stay alive.[1]

I was raised in the 1940s and 1950s in a nonobservant Reform Jewish family. From the time I was a small child, I found that *Something* was there with me during times of confusion or pain. When I got a bit older, old enough to wander our very safe neighborhood alone, I would sometimes go up to the top of a nearby hill and get clarity from encounters with that *Something*.

My family observed a secular Christmas until I was seven years old (safely past the age to learn that no, Virginia, there is *no* Santa Claus). At that time my parents sent me to the Sunday school at our temple. I came home asking why, if we were Jewish, we weren't celebrating the Sabbath and Chanukah (among other Jewish holidays), instead of Christmas. My parents began what seemed an almost embarrassed lighting of Sabbath candles, and we all joyfully switched to the eight days

---

1 Jean Shinoda Bolen, *Crossing to Avalon: A Woman's Midlife Pilgrimage* (San Francisco: HarperSanFrancisco, 1994), 272–73.

of Chanukah—more days for gifts! This was the foundation, for me, of the importance of congruence between one's belief, one's identity, and one's practices and its connection to that *Something*, which I now usually call the Holy One.

Eyes to See: Changing the Narrative

As a teenager I was what I now call a "soft Zionist": that is, one who does not believe that everyone who is Jewish needs to go to live in Israel, but who sees Israel as the only truly "safe" place for Jews in the world. I doubt that I had heard this expression then, but I saw Israel as "a land without people for a people without a land." I believed that the hostile Arabs surrounding it were just ignorant and jealous of the amazing development that Israelis had made in that empty desert into which they had come to live. That was *my* narrative.

I was also incredibly proud of Judaism. Jews were smart, courageous, funny, creative, and among the best of the best. I saw Jews as being in the forefront of everything for which I stood, based on the prophetic tradition of Amos and Isaiah. I knew that two of the three young men killed in Meridian, Mississippi, were Jewish, and that Jews were among those who worked for civil rights and fought for protection of the Bill of Rights.

Sometime after college, I began to realize that people who agreed with me on all the other social issues about which I cared (such as race, gender, sexual orientation, ending war and poverty, and later the earth and our environment) did not necessarily see Palestine/Israel the way that I did. Since there were other issues about which I cared and about which I *was* clear, I just let this one go as too painful, difficult, and confusing to engage.

Many years later, in 2009, my husband, Frank, and I went to Palestine/Israel on a pilgrimage through St. George's College, which is connected with the Anglican Cathedral in Jerusalem. At that time I began to learn a great deal more about what was occurring in Palestine/Israel and its implications. From my youth, I have believed that one of the most courageous and important commitments persons can make is to have the courage to change their positions rather than ignoring or distorting the facts that may conflict with long-held, treasured beliefs. When I came back from the trip, I was led to study and began to follow what was going on in Palestine/Israel, joining a number of groups that enabled me to keep learning.

In October 2013, I had a conversation with Cotton Fite, a retired

Episcopal priest and one of the founders of the Palestine/Israel (P/I) network of the Episcopal Peace Fellowship. While he's had many discouraging moments, he also has hope.

Cotton compared the situation to that in South Africa, which looked utterly hopeless prior to Nelson Mandela's release from prison. There, world opinion was central to change, leading to the successful movement of boycott, divestment, and sanctions (BDS), largely initiated by the commitment of people of faith throughout the United States and Europe. Our narrative about the situation in Palestine/Israel is also changeable. Because of the relationship between Israel and the United States, the church and other organizations can play an important role in changing the narrative here, which could shift American foreign policy, as it did toward South Africa.

Sometime shortly after talking with Cotton, I received invitations to consider a trip to Palestine/Israel from several of the groups, including the Compassionate Listening Project (CLP). CLP was founded by Leah Green, a Jewish woman from Washington State, largely using Quaker principles learned from her Quaker mentor, Gene Hoffman. Gene spent two years in France studying with Thich Nhat Hanh.

The Compassionate Listening organization takes groups from various countries to Palestine/Israel, teaches them the processes of Compassionate Listening, and introduces them to a wide variety of individuals, with opportunities to listen in some depth.

My life was changed by that 2014 trip.

At the end of each time of listening on the trip, we had opportunities to ask open and honest questions, that is, questions with no right or wrong answer and to which we could anticipate the answer we would receive.

We spoke with Shaul Yudelman, an Orthodox (Hasidic) Jew who lives in a West Bank settlement, and Ziad Sabateen, a Muslim former participant in the intifadas and prisoner of the Israeli Defense Force for five years,

I said, "I would like to ask each of you the same question: If you were given absolute power as emperor of this land, what would you do?" Their answers shocked, informed, and challenged me. Both of them said that if he had the power to make the other's people disappear from what each called "my people's land," they would, because "this is our land." However, they each were quick to acknowledge that both peoples are there and are not going to go away. So, each believes they are called to live out the very same values each learned through his own respective religious tradition, and to learn to live at peace with their neighbors.

Would that we could do that here at home. While I am not able to make any difference in diplomatic talks between Israel and Palestine, I am able to share my understandings here with people who can, in turn, influence others and thus public opinion in general. Since my visits, I've been reading and networking, writing and speaking, and I continue to remain open to how else I might learn and grow in my own understanding and narrative.

How does the situation in Palestine/Israel and the importance of revising our own narratives feature in a book on dismantling racism?

A major lesson for me has been that *it's all of us or none*. If all of us are not *we* rather than *us and them*, none of us is safe, physically, emotionally, or morally. The poem "First They Came" by the German pastor Martin Niemöller makes the same point in its powerful description of the process of the result of an us and them mentality.[2]

The work that I do for the purpose of reconciliation is not just to benefit the one who is oppressed, but to allow me to look for and hope for and work for the opportunity to live in a world in which there are no outsiders. My own mental, spiritual, intellectual, and political health is dependent, at least in part, on my working to close the Tragic Gap (as Parker Palmer names it), resisting the temptation to move away from or ignore it.

We who benefit from White privilege need to take responsibility to learn what we do not know, and to take action to level the playing field where we are able. It is a humbling, if not humiliating process. But it is not all or nothing. So to my White sisters and brothers I say, take heart. We're all works in progress. But remember, *we do need to do the work*.

Theological Reflections on Hope

After returning from Palestine/Israel in 2014, I spoke first at a gathering cosponsored by a local church, the Colorado Chapter of the Episcopal Peace Fellowship (EPF), and the Colorado branch of Friends of Sabeel North America (FOSNA). Mary Ellen Garrett, a member of our EPF Colorado steering committee, and I worked together on this.

Shortly before the event, the Israeli Defense Force began the bombing of Gaza, killing many civilians, including the elderly, women, and children, and laying such waste to infrastructure that pictures of it reminded me of photos I'd seen of Dresden after World War II.

I had come back with so many stories full of hope, but this seemed

---

2 Pastor Martin Niemöller, "First They Came," Holocaust Memorial Day Trust, http://hmd. org.uk/resources/poetry/first-they-came-pastor-martin-niemöller.

to auger something frighteningly unhopeful. During a planning lunch, Mary Ellen gave me, in effect, a sermon on hope, pointing out that this Christian virtue is absolutely necessary, especially in times of trial. She may have mentioned the line from Hebrews 11:1: "Now faith is the assurance of things hoped for, the conviction of things not seen." Somehow it was just the salve I needed, the impetus to continue working for peace and justice in Palestine, no matter how things looked. The encouragement did not go just one way. Sometime not long after that lunch, another awful event happened in Palestine, and this time Mary Ellen was distraught and feeling hopeless. I reminded her that she is the ambassador of hope for me, and I was able to give the gift back to her. We need each other to be able to continue in hope, working for peace and justice in the Beloved Community. And we need to allow ourselves to feel the grief and tension of living in the Tragic Gap.

We can allow ourselves to be so discouraged by difficult, apparently intractable conditions that we lose hope. As a painful but illustrative example in our own country's racial saga, the story of the four young girls killed by racist bombers in 1963 at the 16th Street Baptist Church in Birmingham could, on the one hand, be used as proof that hatred wins. Yet we might also find hope there, for in looking at the impact it had on changing attitudes, even such tragic loss can become the impetus for movement forward. I believe that recent events across our country are leading to a change in the narrative both of our nation's media and its White citizens. Even in the midst of this deep pain, hope happens.

I am heartened by two recent events in Denver, where I live. First, a few months after the tragic shooting at Mother Emanuel AME Church in Charleston, South Carolina, Shorter AME Church (a large Denver congregation) held an interfaith service for racial healing and reconciliation. One of the singing groups was Sikh. The leader of that group spoke powerfully of his gratitude for being included in this event, the first time he and his community had ever been invited to be part of another religious community's worship. The gathered group was amazingly diverse, and our diversity added to the sense that something important, healing, and hope-filled was happening. It surely was an experience of Beloved Community.

My own congregation, a downtown, smallish-but-growing Episcopal parish, has been actively involved in social justice issues for decades, but has focused primarily on the rights of the LGBTQ community and services to the homeless, including efforts to reintegrate homeless persons into the mainstream. We recently started two groups to work on aspects of racial reconciliation. I believe the impetus for this was coverage of recent tragedies around the country, combined with media exposure of local injustices at the Denver jail.

My favorite Bible verse has become Romans 8:28, my favorite translation of which reads: "In all things God works together *with us* for good." St. Augustine believed that while we cannot act without God, God will not act without us. For people of faith, our part is not insignificant. Our willingness to step forward and to ask God to use us is essential to move our hearts to action. My understanding is that God's answer shows up as a nudge or a sense of call. If this understanding is correct, our "yes, please" is a necessary component of our ability to make a contribution to justice, to healing, and to the growth of the Beloved Community.

Dueling Narratives

In Palestine it became clear to me that what sustained the intractable conflict was not so much the facts as the way narratives have varied. In both Palestine/Israel and within the United States, our inability to consider the narrative, the suffering, the fear, of the Other creates a lens through which the Other is invisible, inferior. Often our enemies are found to be people whose stories we have not heard and who have deep wounds that can lead to violent actions. When we put forth an effort to understand those who we see as Other, it is easier to find compassion for them instead of judgment.

When we can listen deeply to a narrative at odds with the one we have created out of our experiences, the possibility of growth and change—the possibility of Beloved Community—is present in the tension. Since Israelis and White Americans have such power in these situations, they also hold much of the responsibility to find ways to respond with justice.

Whenever there is conflict, and an inability to see each other as fully human, peace becomes impossible. It is easier to support a hostile narrative when people on either side of the divide do not have opportunities to see and get to know each other. While I was in Israel, many of the people we met did not know one member of the other side. Note that this is also true in the United States for many Blacks and Whites.

The Relationship between Inner Work and Our Work in the World

Parker Palmer, the Quaker writer and educator based at the Center for Courage and Renewal, leads people toward the goal of congruence between soul and role.

One of Palmer's images is the Mobius strip.[3] One takes a narrow strip of paper that is of two colors, one on each side. One side represents the inner self, the other the self presented to the world. For much of our lives, at least for many of us, the ends of the strip are glued together in such a way that a circle is formed, the inside of which is one color, the outside a second. Much of what is on the inside is kept hidden from the world.

But another way is to twist the ends before attaching them so that the sides with the two colors come together at the ends, and the strip forms a figure eight. Then, following the edge of the strip, it starts with one color and inexorably leads to the other. Doing good soul work leads one to move out into the world and live what one has learned from soul. It leads to integrity and a sense of wholeness. And working in the world inexorably calls us back to soul work.

As Palmer uses the notion of soul, it is that "still small voice"[4] that the Quakers call the "inner light," that may be understood as the Holy Spirit, that is the source of guidance and mystery and wholeness to which inner work attunes us. Role is the way we engage in the world—as teacher, child, parent, friend, community organizer, ad infinitum.

Tools for Inner Work

I have come to believe that the inner journey takes us out of the absolute center of our own universe in such a way that our gifts and talents are available for the building of Beloved Community, in which all are welcome, all are honored, all are loved.

We are born self-centered. This is not a condemnation, but a developmental fact. Some folks stay there all their lives, while some blessed folks actually reach the point where all humanity is part of "us."

All the world's major religions address these issues. Those of us in the Christian spiritual tradition have Jesus's commandments to love God and one's neighbor, the latter being anyone in need, through whom we serve Jesus himself.[5] Many branches of Judaism speak of *Tikkun Olam*, or the healing of the world. Buddhism teaches that some folks, called Bodhisattvas once they have reached enlightenment, choose to hang around rather than pass on to nirvana not because of any need of their own, but simply to be of service.

I believe there are many tools for this work, including the heroes and

---

3   Parker Palmer, *A Hidden Wholeness: The Journey Toward an Undivided Life* (San Francisco: Jossey-Bass, 2004), chap. 3.

4   1 Kings 19:12.

5   Mark 12:30–31; Matthew 25:31–46.

heroines who provide us with characteristics to emulate; journaling our thoughts, feelings, experiences, and dreams; spiritual direction as an aide in discernment; meditation and contemplation; and forgiveness (which is distinct from forgetfulness or reconciliation).

There are many models for a contemplative practice, and lots of popular articles as well as information on controlled research. My own experience is that, combined with other spiritual practices, my form of contemplative practice (called Centering Prayer) has helped me to grow in self-awareness, to decrease in judgment of myself and others, to grow in compassion, and to be present to what is going on in the *now* of my life. While it comes from the Benedictine (more specifically Trappist) community, and has roots in fourteenth-century England, Centering Prayer is free of doctrine or any particular theological position, so is useful for anyone interested in spiritual growth. It's being taught in prisons, in business and industry, and many other social locations in our society in addition to churches and retreat centers.

I have practiced Centering Prayer for over thirty years. Working with the Compassionate Listening Project, I learned something new that has enhanced the practice. They call it "breathing through the heart."

This practice seems to be helping me to be both more open, and less triggered by events which at one time would have been terribly upsetting and would have carried me to deep anger and judgment against others. And the capacity to stay in this peaceful center often seems to carry over from prayer time to regular time. When you feel judgmental or defensive, it helps to ask yourself how the persons creating that reaction in you have come to be who they are and what you can learn about yourself from your response to them.

For a number of years I have offered retreats and workshops on the topic of forgiveness. I have come to believe that the ability to understand and work through forgiveness is a major key to happiness, to mental and spiritual health, and to well-being. It is certainly a necessary component of conflict resolution and the creation of Beloved Community.

The major obstacle I see to forgiving is a misunderstanding of what it is and what it means. Here are some of the issues:

Forgiveness is not forgetting. If we could forget the offense, it wouldn't need to be forgiven.

Forgiveness is not condoning. If the offense were excusable, it wouldn't need to be forgiven.

Forgiveness is not reconciliation. The former is a one person job. The latter is a two person job, and requires repentance and amendment of life from the offender in order to be safe for the person mistreated.

Forgiveness is not about the offender. It is really about you and your freedom.

Forgiveness is not about the past, but about redeeming the future.

Forgiveness is always of individuals, never of actions.

Forgiveness can best perhaps be understood through some metaphors. One, attributed to Nelson Mandela among others, is, "Refusing forgiveness is like taking poison and expecting it to kill the other person."

The process does not require that you have all your feelings ducks lined up in a row. Forgiveness at heart is not so much a change of feelings. Rather *forgiveness is a decision;* the feelings often shift *afterward*.

One version of the Lord's Prayer says, "Forgive us our debts as we forgive our debtors." Once, after being constantly angry and feeling impotent at an unpaid literal debt owed me, I wrote the offender and said, "If you ever decide to pay me back, it will be a Christmas present. As of now, you owe me nothing; the debt is cancelled." Finally able to put the letter into the mail box and let it go, a process which required several iterations, I confess, I walked away feeling like I was floating. A great lesson, pretty cheaply earned. And one thing about the debt image—if it's *forgiven,* you can't renege and take the money back. If the feelings haven't come along, or occasionally return, remind yourself that that's another issue.

Models for Groups Working across Differences

Other chapters in this book will cover in depth a number of models for safely working through issues of human difference. Here are a few that I have found effective and helpful.[6]

The National Coalition Building Institute (NCBI)

Perhaps the most unexpected shift in understanding of diversity which has come to me was at a one day workshop I took a number of years ago with Cherie Brown, founder and director of the National Coalition Building Institute. There is an inclusivity in the NCBI understanding of diversity which I have found unique, and which was exciting and empowering to experience.

---

6   Two other models you might wish to check out:
- Restorative Justice—bringing together offenders and victims of crime; allowing them each to share their stories; providing methods of making amends. Government cooperation is necessary. For more information, see http://www.restorativejustice.org.
- Nonviolent Communication (NVC)—sometimes called Compassionate Communication, this method of conflict resolution was developed by Marshall Rosenberg. For resources, history, and methodology, see https://www.cnvc.org/about/what-is-nvc.html.

Quaker Heritage: Circles of Trust, Alternatives to Violence, and Compassionate Listening

I believe that Quakers are the most convincing witnesses in our country of the importance of both the inner and the outer work and their inner connection. Traditional Quakers do not have clergy, are nonhierarchical, and spend much of their communal time in silence, both in prayer meetings and in business meetings.

Yet they have not retreated from the world. Rather, Quakers have contributed to racial justice and nonviolent resistance to injustice in ways that are hard to imagine, given how small their numbers. Take just one example: many of the most important leaders in the abolition movement were Quakers. For a compelling role model, see the journals of John Woolman, available in many versions.

Circles of Trust, Alternatives to Violence, and Compassionate Listening have Quaker roots and offer a value which is rarely seen elsewhere in our dominant American culture, namely that the goal of conversation is to understand every position rather than to convince. They have been used quite effectively in prison work.

The Importance of Covenant

As we create safe space in groups, the absolute importance of covenant should be addressed. In any group (two or more persons) there is always a covenant, sometimes unspoken, but with negative consequences if it is transgressed. The larger the group, and the more difficult the work, the greater the need to be clear on its covenant or agreement. There are idiosyncratic elements in every covenant, but some issues which I believe need to be included are agreements on goals, keeping confidentiality, timeliness and time-keeping, and processes for decision-making, action, and consensus.

Discernment on Leaning into the Light

If you don't know where you might be called to help create the Beloved Community, my suggestion is that you pray to be shown, indicate your willingness, and then pay attention—especially watching for coincidences.

I have come to believe that the most useful petitionary prayer is the Serenity Prayer. The key is the third petition.

God, grant me the serenity to accept
　the things I cannot change,
The courage to change the things I can,
And the wisdom to know the difference.[7]

　As you are discerning that call, study, pray for guidance, watch for coincidences, ask others for help, step out into the new, and remember that you are not alone.

7　Reinhold Niebuhr and Robert McAfee Brown, *The Essential Reinhold Niebuhr: Selected Essays* (Binghamton, NY: Vail-Ballou Press, 1986), 251.

8 The American South Is Our Holy Land

Robert C. Wright

"I took my family to the Holy Land some time ago . . . you ever been?" That's how I usually start telling the story. "You know the Holy Land . . . Alabama, Mississippi, Tennessee . . . Georgia?" After I say that, mostly there is polite laughter and smiles that acknowledge, "Hey, that was kind of clever, never heard that one before." Some people make a hybrid noise, the "laugh/hmmmmmmphs." Preachers know that noise best as an affirmation. The noise people make when something you've said registers as resembling the truth. The "laugh/hmmmmph" is the noise people make when something you've said tickles some, but punches more. I don't remember the first time I said it, the thing about the American South being the Holy Land. It came from somewhere beyond my head up to my mouth, but I'm sure it was before the trip. Beth, my wife, and I took our four little children from Atlanta where we live, up to Lookout Mountain, Tennessee, the very same one mentioned in the "I Have a Dream" speech, and down to Memphis to the Lorraine Motel where Dr. King stopped breathing. From there we headed south. Down to Jackson, Mississippi, across the Tallahatchie River, where they tried to erase Emmett Till. From there the family trip went over to Selma across the Alabama River via the Edmund Pettus Bridge. If you've never seen that bridge in person, know this: it's smaller than it looks on film. On film it looks long like the Chesapeake Bay Bridge or the Lake Ponchatrain Bridge of Louisiana, both snaking spans of many miles. In person, the Edmund Pettus Bridge is overwhelmingly small. Just 1,248 feet. That's it! Just like what people say about Jerusalem and Bethlehem. The places loom large but are actually very small. What looms large in my mind about walking over that bridge with my wife and children, my youngest riding on my shoulders, was what had been placed on the Montgomery side of the bridge, which is the eastern shore of the river. There were stones. Twelve of them. More like boulders actually. Old, knowing stones. The central stone cries out in words from a distant holy land. The text is from the Bible, where else?

> When your children ask their parents in time to come, "What do these stones mean?" then you shall let your children know, "Israel crossed over the Jordan here on dry ground." (Josh. 4:21–22)

Back into the car and on to Montgomery, Alabama, and the Dexter Avenue Baptist Church. The whole way from Selma to Montgomery, Beth and I were pointing out to the children, "and the marchers would have still been walking. Still be walking—yep, still walking." An Exodus. Bondage breaking exertion. I really wanted to get to Dexter Avenue Baptist Church. Really! Not so much for the sanctuary as for the parsonage. The sanctuary was nice. Quaint. Like thousands of churches all over the south. Dexter Avenue Church was where King preached his just-out-of-graduate-school sermons. The right stuff. Eloquent. Theologically sound, but as one matriarch of the church confided in us, "just ok." But it was the parsonage where Coretta and their first child, Yolanda, were almost blown up that interested me. We paused there at the front steps to see where the dynamite had been placed, just before Coretta randomly left the front room and took the baby to the back of the house. If hate leaves a stain, then that corner of their front stoop is forever stained. What I wanted to see most in Montgomery was King's kitchen table in that parsonage. Sounds funny but that table was the one where he prayed over a cup of coffee at a particularly dark midnight for him personally and in terms of the bus boycott. In the late evening after a meeting, King answers his telephone only to hear threats for him and his wife and infant child. "I am going to kill you and your family if you don't get out of town." It was 1956. You don't sleep after that. You prepare for a long night. You reach for coffee. You sit. His kitchen table is where he said he ended up. No comfort in the coffee. But at that table he said he heard from God. That

God met him in his faltering faith that night and promised him that if he stood up for justice and righteousness that God would be with him and never leave or forsake him. He would repeat that story often in sermons. For me, seeing that table meant that I had seen the second sitting down of the civil rights movement that changed everything. The first was, of course, Rosa Parks's strategic sit-down on a bus. This sit-down was for Martin's confession and prayer. Both of their sit-downs led to so much standing up all around the country but particularly in the South. That table conjures that up for me. That table whispers to me Jeremiah's recollection of God's words to him:

> But the LORD said to me,
>
> "Do not say, 'I am only a boy';
> for you shall go to all to whom I send you,
> and you shall speak whatever I command you.
> Do not be afraid of them,
> for I am with you to deliver you,
> says the LORD."
>
> Then the LORD put out his hand and touched my mouth;
> and the LORD said to me,
>
> "Now I have put my words in your mouth.
>
> See, today I appoint you over nations and over kingdoms,
> to pluck up and to pull down,
> to destroy and to overthrow,
> to build and to plant." (Jer. 1:7–10)

The trip ended when we arrived back home in Atlanta. Back home to where Martin and Coretta are resting in an embarrassingly poorly maintained King Center and where Andrew Young and C. T. Vivian are still working on souls, their own included. Back home to the city that maintains as its mantra, "The city too busy to hate." Beth and I resumed our hectic lives. But, we had seen something. Been somewhere special. Not the special you feel from seeing important artifacts. But the special you feel when you see an old family photo album of relatives you never knew. Special like discovering your ancestry.

II.

Wisdom sits in places.

—Apache proverb

*Some parts of space are qualitatively different
from others.*

—Mircea Eliade

Maybe we should back up and slow down. Maybe the traditional understanding of the phrase Holy Land can better shed some light on what I am trying to convey. When most people talk about the Holy Land, they are referring to land roughly located between the Jordan River and the Mediterranean Sea, including the eastern bank of the Jordan River. The land there is considered holy by certain Jews, Christians, and Muslims because each of these great faiths have patriarchs and matriarchs who profess to having met and consorted with God on this land. So then the land means something extraordinary. The land is geo-theological—holy geology and geography—which is the location where both the personal and communal experience of God in past days occurred. The place where significance and guidance for present-day actions abound, in addition to the sense of the promise of continued relationship, identity, and even prosperity in the future with God. It's all about the identity of people. And, to one degree or the other, a holy land is about mitigating the fear of the vastness of the universe by the coziness that comes from knowing God in a particular place over time. The land is holy because labor and pain, joy and grief, birth and death, war and peace, prayer to and betrayal of God have happened on this land and therefore it is set apart. It knows and is deeply known. As the Buddhists say, the place has a "suchness" about it—comfortable in its own skin and at home with its own nature. On holy land, people have been beguiled and inspired. Calmed and stirred. Saved and forsaken. Even experienced bliss enough to breathe deeply and know clearly, if only for an instant, the better and most full sense of life.

The Celts and later Celtic Christian term for places that are uniquely endowed with the divine is "thin" places. The term is used for rare locales where the distance between heaven and earth collapses. That is, where a place for a myriad of reasons has the ability to reveal the mind of eternity. A place where time gives way to timelessness and where partiality gives way to fluidity as the truest reality. Could this be what St. Paul meant when in his soliloquy on love in his first letter to a congregation in Corinth he said,

> For now we see in a mirror, dimly, but then we will see face to face. Now I know only in part; then I will know fully, even as I have been fully known. (1 Cor. 13:12–13)

Could it have been that in Corinth Paul was prompted to write these words because of the location? Had location collapsed the dividing line between heaven and earth, if only momentarily? There are other Bible stories that point to this phenomena. Maybe it happened in the conversation between Abraham and God that climaxes in Abraham's upward gaze at the stars. Then there is Jacob's dream of angels ascending and descending. Much later in the book, we hear of travelers from the East, commonly called the wise men, as they follow their star and find their hearts' longing. We could be seeing it in Mary's faith and the exchange between her and the propositioning angel Gabriel. And I believe we see it in Jesus's crucifixion moment. As he breathes his last and dies, the words spoken by a standing Roman soldier were, "Truly this man was the son of God." People, moments, and places. Heaven and earth collapsing, showing their finely woven shared fabric. Revealing the true. Unmasking reality. They say that in thin places, we become our more essential selves. Maybe that is the chief gift of holy land: it's ability to tell truth without language. To lay bare. To take away falsehood and half truths about the nature of life and society and to give an enlivening, eternal sense of reality that inspires awe, humility, boldness, and connectedness all at the same time. In the Holy Land, in what we call the Middle East and here, in the American Deep South, we know that God confuses as much as confirms. That God through particular locations helps us to lose our moorings so we can find new ones. That the human pattern is that we have to be jolted out of old ways of seeing the world and one another to really see. And maybe wherever that happens is holy. And if that happens frequently in a particular place, we could call that place holy land. There is a residue of something holy and real, awful and awe-inspiring in the American South—the cities and the fields—that is speaking to us, if we are inclined to listen.

III.

He drew me up from the desolate pit,
out of the miry bog,
and set my feet upon a rock,
  making my steps secure.
He put a new song in my mouth. . . .

—Psalm 40:2–3

I started thinking about all of this growing up as a biracial child in Pittsburgh, Pennsylvania. There was always this story of race all around me: the story of Africans in America. Slavery in the American South. The fight for human dignity and civil rights. And whatever comes after civil rights. The story that God would make a way. That if God intervened wonderfully over there, in the Holy Land, then God would continue to intervene over here. How could God not, there are so many parallels? I believed it. I believe it. The South is America's Holy Land. What one story can I give to bring this idea home? Not one "anything" could do that. To make the point, you need stories and songs. You need long stories with laughter and tears from old people with holes in their recollections. Stories that are told with long, descriptive silences.

But stories alone can't flesh this thing out. Facts don't fly high enough or reach deep enough. Poetry riding on melody is necessary. As the psalmist asked, "How could we sing the LORD's song in a foreign land?" (137:4). But they found a way in this Holy Land. Way back it was the psalmists from the Fisk Jubilee singers of Nashville, Tennessee. "Oh, the rocks and the mountains shall all flee away, And you shall have a new hiding place that day." Then there was Mahalia Jackson singing *Come Sunday,* accompanied by Duke Ellington, reminding us gray skies come, but they're just passing by . . . there's a brighter light on high. Then there is the haunting whine of Lady Day, Ms. Billie Holiday. Part of her whine gives voice to the chilling idea of trees dripping with black male bodies and the mourning of too many mothers . . . Strange Fruit in the trees, a scene from the "gallant South" she says. Some of her whine is her own self-loathing. But, either way, only she can sing *Strange Fruit* for me.

Then there is Eunice Kathleen Waymon or, as we know her, Nina Simone. A daughter of the South—Tryon, North Carolina—and the high priestess of soul. With her voice, songs, and celebrity, she responded to the murder of Medgar Evers and the church bombing in Birmingham, Alabama, that killed four little black girls and blinded a fifth girl who survived with the song *Mississippi Goddam!* No exposition necessary.

And why did Ray Charles sing so lovingly about Georgia anyway? Why is Georgia on Ray's mind? We know the song was originally written and performed by Hoagy Carmichael in 1930. It was allegedly about his sister who he was very fond of. But the song only became a chart topper in 1960 when Charles put Carmichael's words through his southern soul. It is fair to say that Ray's not singing about Carmichael's sister when he sings Georgia on my mind. His rendition feels like one part lament, one part hope. To my ear, his voice holds together a faint tone of sarcasm and a visceral longing for the words of the song to be really, really true. His Georgia is a sweet old song and a relationship that causes him to refuse the other arms that reach out.

What does he connect to in those words? We can't ever really know. We do know that one year after Charles released his version of the song, it climbed the charts. But in the very next year, Charles canceled a concert scheduled to take place in the Bell Auditorium in Augusta, Georgia, to protest against segregated seating. We know that Charles did have to pay $800 in compensation to the promoter for that cancellation. We know that, according to the New Georgia Encyclopedia, there were 458 victims of lynchings in Georgia, only to be exceeded by the state of Mississippi at 538. At one point in the state's history, Georgia averaged more than one mob killing a month. We know that at the height of Ray Charles's career, the people of Georgia elected a renowned segregationist, Lester Maddox, to be its governor. Maddox, in response to the 1964 Civil Rights Act, famously closed his Pickrick southern cuisine restaurant rather than serve black customers. With all of this in the air in Georgia, what makes Ray Charles sing, "Georgia, a song of you comes as sweet and clear as moonlight through the pines . . . "? Charles's song about Georgia and maybe the whole South sounds like the complicated *I love you* whispered to the lover who has broken your heart. We need the songbirds and the players of instruments to help us understand something about this holy land. Hope and heartbreak are the best partners for writing and arranging songs.

IV.

I will open my mouth in a parable;
  I will utter dark sayings from of old,
  things that we have heard and known,
    that our ancestors have told us.
  We will not hide them from their children.

—Psalm 78:2–4

Maybe this whole notion touched me more than it should have being born in 1964 because my parents were fifty years older than my sister and me. They adopted the two of us. Two biracial babies for two fifty-year-olds. Both of them domestics, neither having more than a fourth grade education. Earl born in 1912, Charlene in 1913. Both in October. They had lived through so much. Heard and seen so much. They still knew the words that had come up from the South. The sayings. They knew the songs. They passed on to us both the soundtrack and the script, the way every parent passes on songs and scripts. Each in their own way: Earl in his frustrated, drunk, impeccably manicured, hard-working, quiet, presentation of himself to the world. Charlene, through her secrets, elegance, and her profound sadness that came out every time she sat down to play the organ, either at home or at St. Benedict the Moor Catholic Church. The church with the sculpture of a black man, 120 feet up, 18 feet tall, and 14 feet wide, weighing 3,000 pounds. The church and the statue are still standing today. Because of that congregation, from whose orphanage I was plucked by Earl and Charlene, I grew up with images of a Jesus with sun-kissed skin. Because of my parents, their delights, defects, and demons, my sister and I learned that God was involved with America and her people. Especially those who have labored and been oppressed. Especially the ones who have suffered unspeakable and unfathomable violence to their dignity. My parents' day-to-day reality, as laborers to very affluent, white families, was one of Pharaoh and Moses. David and Goliath. Judas and Jesus. Stories about how God was for us. That God was for anybody that was "buked and scorned." That everybody talking about heaven wasn't going there. And that someday God would intervene in the real world and as the Negro spiritual says "all God's children would have shoes and they would walk all over God's heaven." Even though we lived in Pittsburgh, Pennsylvania, and had never traveled South, with limited real knowledge of the South, the South was our Jerusalem. The Carolinas, Alabama, Georgia, Mississippi, down to Florida and over to Louisiana—that is where the struggle for freedom, dignity, sanity, and soul had its epicenter.

It was in the air somehow: on that bridge over there, in that church right there. Down that road over there, plantations were populated and planted. In those fields, resolve was strengthened. We knew, if only at a distance, Bible verses were recited down there. Africa was remembered. Songs were composed. Language was developed. Humor was applied as medicine. Genius was multiplied. In that grove of old oak trees was where we were afraid, tied, beaten, raped, and castrated. Down there is the saw grass, cotton, tobacco, and rice fields. Down there rape and redemption were siblings. Down there sin, songs, and sermons lived side by side. Oglethorpe's sermons liberated. Whitfield's sermons enslaved. Down there where Goliath and David still did their dance. Down South evil giants like George Wallace, Bull Connor, Byron De La Beckwith, and Sheriff Jim Clark prowled the land. Down there were cowards that covered their faces and stalked women and children by night like serpents. Down there black bodies hung from trees like Spanish moss, just like crosses littered Roman city roads in Jesus's day. Down there the body parts of lynched men were passed around like party favors to bloodthirsty crowds.

But what redeems all this, what makes it all that is grotesque about the South's fodder for the holy is that evil is the necessary precondition for good. Esther confronted and defeated her Haman, Moses his Pharaoh, David his Goliath. Each with their flesh proved God's bias for justice. We see this in the South as well. Teenaged champions like the high-schoolers in Birmingham that cut school to shred segregation. College kids in Nashville sitting at lunch counters, enduring blows and allowing their ears to be used as ash trays for burning cigarettes. We don't know their names, but we know the names of some of the champions like Claudette Colvin, Mary Louise Smith, Rosa Parks, Violet Liuzzo, Ella Baker, Marian Wright Edelman, Coretta Scott King, Jean Childs Young, Fred Shuttlesworth, Bob Moses, Charles Hamilton Houston, Vernon Johns, Johnathan Daniels, Diane Nash, C. T. Vivian, and Jim Lawson. Then there were the champions who we knew by one name—Orange, Farmer, King, Andy, Thurgood, Rustin, and Bevel. And those are just some of the names we know. It boggles the mind to think about the multitude of people who through minuscule militant acts contended with evil and found God mighty to save.

Yes, of course, I know other regions of the nation participated in and profited from American chattel slavery—centuries of stolen personhood, stolen labor, and squandered human potential. Yes, of course, other regions of this great country have struggled mightily and birthed saints out of sinfulness. We can't minimize that. No states or regions of this country are free and clear from benefitting from the four hundred years of free labor and intellectual property of the Africans brought to this country to make its claims on prosperity real. We know this increasingly through important work like *Traces of the Trade: A Story from the Deep North,* which chronicles the assent of one New England family, the DeWolf family, who rose up through the ranks of business, religion, politics, and high society as a result of being the most prolific slavers in the United States. From 1769 to 1820, DeWolf fathers, sons, and grandsons trafficked in human beings. They sailed their ships from Bristol, Rhode Island, to West Africa with rum to trade for African men, women, and children. Captives were taken to plantations that the DeWolfs owned in Cuba or were sold at auction in such ports as Havana and Charleston. Sugar and molasses were then brought from Cuba to the family-owned rum distilleries in Bristol. Over the generations, the family transported more than ten thousand enslaved Africans across the Middle Passage. They amassed an enormous fortune. By the end of his life, James DeWolf had been a US Senator and was reportedly the second richest man in the United States.[1]

Yet with all of that being true, and many more stories yet to be told about the Deep North's contribution to slavery, there is something about the American South's role in all of that. I admit it's hard to put your finger on. There's something unique. Something ancient. Like the knowing Mississippi River. Rolling. Slow but not dead. It has to do with blood and faith. Sin and salvation. Hate and love locked in relationship as family. Locked in active struggle. Down South. At least in my mind, in my emotions, even in my spirit, down South is the American Holy Land. And I know I am not the only one.

---

1 *Traces of the Trade: A Story from the Deep North,* http://www.tracesofthetrade.org/synopsis.

CHAPTER 6

9 Getting Dismantling Racism Right in Atlanta

Beth King and Catherine Meeks

Catherine

The 2000 General Convention of The Episcopal Church passed a resolution that required participation in antiracism training for all who hold any leadership role within the church. In compliance with that resolution, the Diocese of Atlanta formed an Anti-Racism Commission as part of their commitment to the work. For several years the training was conducted using a corporate model along with the materials that had been incorporated in *Seeing God's Face in Each Other,* provided by The Episcopal Church. The primary work of the Anti-Racism Commission was focused around training and as the years passed, it became more difficult to get those individuals who were required to participate to sign up. Finally the training came to a halt and for several months there was no training in the diocese. Three years ago, Robert Wright was elected as the 10th bishop of the diocese. It was time to get the program back on track; this time it was not just for compliance sake: there was critical work that needed to be done.

The chair was retiring from his profession and was ready to retire from the Commission as well and I, as a longtime member of the Commission with great passion in the work, was invited to become the chair. Under new leadership and with encouragement from Bishop Wright, the Commission took up the task of changing its name to "Beloved Community: Commission for Dismantling Racism." Bishop Wright had suggested that the name should speak to the work the Commission was charged to do. This was a welcome shift following years when many in the diocese had objected to the previous name and the Commission had been hesitant to change it. With a new chair and a new bishop, the time was finally right and the change was enthusiastically embraced by all of the members of the Commission.

Along with the name change, the Commission began a major campaign to create more visibility for its work, expanding its vision to include more than training events. Parishes were encouraged to become involved in book studies, film programs, and discussions on the issues of race in their respective locales. For three years the Commission has organized and sponsored bus trips to Hayneville, Alabama, for the Jonathan Daniels Pilgrimages, a diocesan-wide Repentance and Reconciliation Service attended by almost eight hundred people, a conversation on race involving local and national church leaders, a one-day conference on Howard Thurman that brought people from around the country, and the passing of a resolution in 2015 reaffirming our commitment to the General Convention Resolution of 2000. The recent diocesan resolution mandates that all activities related to dismantling racism be reported to the Commission, allowing a comprehensive report of efforts across the diocese. The resolution also encourages the ongoing use of the dismantling racism training in those parishes where it has not been fully implemented.

The training, which continues to be a major part of the work, went through quite a transformation. We moved from a corporate model of training to Eucharist-centered dismantling racism training. It is that story that we now tell.

Beth

Because Catherine and I had never met, it was a little tricky. Scanning the room where we were to meet for lunch, I did a quick evaluation of possible individuals. Catherine had arrived first and I could see she was doing the same scan. "Catherine?" I inquired. "Yes. Beth?" she ventured. "Yes. Thank God you're Black!" I blurted out. Although a novice, I knew that diversity would be a key element. It was an odd beginning but in some ways prophetic. The connection was instantaneous. We each recognized in the other something needed to make this partnership come together; and we haven't slowed down since. To state that Catherine has been a tremendous mentor is a gross understatement. I feel privileged to sit at her feet.

This beginning led to deeper conversations about the training classes but also—and just as important—about where each of us was on this path of reconciliation work. It would take a great deal of trust and nuanced understanding of each other to stand before twenty to twenty-five individuals and lead them through the work of facing very difficult topics. It is here that trainers must model the trust and respect they are asking of participants. Catherine and I allowed the time to question one another about perspectives with true listening. It would be evident later how vitally important true listening is. These conversations also revealed the gifts each of us brought to this process and how best to use them. The important and hard work of helping individuals become the Beloved Community would take not just skill as facilitators but spirit, heart, and commitment.

The next challenge was to design the training to persuade others to accept this commitment also. In this day, participants are guided to remember and embrace their baptismal covenant: "Will you strive for justice and peace among all people, and respect the dignity of every human being?" "I will, with God's help" (BCP, 305). Beginning the day's work with Holy Eucharist unfurls the umbrella that will cover all that follows as we discuss living out this covenant. The impact has been powerful and substantial. At times it has even been surprisingly revelatory to those attending the class. Before a word has been spoken within the training itself, a mindset has been altered. Addressing racism now becomes personal. It is an integral part of each one's spiritual life. It is done as part of one's participation in the body of Christ—not just on behalf of the "other."

It is important to be prepared to meet people where they are on their journey. However impatient we might be to get everyone to the ever-elusive state of reconciliation, it is imperative to recognize that individuals are unique and trainers must be able to greet each one at their location.

For some, especially people of color, it may feel like a waste of time. They have seen these attempts before without results. Very often it was something done to placate. At the very least it is lame, at its worst, deceptive. Whites, too, anticipate a waste of precious time and are resistant to any suggestion that they might discover a new, changed appreciation for the "other" in their world. In both scenarios folks have walked away from the potential gift of transformation. They have left on the table, unwrapped, the gift of an encounter with the divine by not seeing the face of God in all people. We all need to be nudged a little further down the road without being run over.

I have always felt a kinship with the Celtic saints, especially St. Aidan. David Adam, former vicar of Holy Island (Lindisfarne), invites us to see Aidan approaching people wherever they happen to be at that moment.[1] His was never an anticipation of waiting for them to rise to his level of spirituality or enlightenment. In the same manner we need be patient enough to engage participants where they are, regardless of our own understanding of this very difficult and highly charged subject. No one ever said it would be easy. Trainers are faced with the task of bringing White participants from a self-perception that they are not racist to accepting the realities of White privilege—avoiding blame, shame, guilt, finally moving toward acceptance and reconciliation. This is no small shift in people's life lens or self-image in eight hours. Equally critical is bringing Black participants to a place of understanding and willingness to see God's face in those who are often not seen as equals.

To expect that anything like this can happen, certain priorities for the day have to be established. Participants are asked to commit to several principles for the day, the first being respect. That respect applies not only to individual personalities but to the stories, perspectives, and beliefs that are shared no matter how offensive or contrary to another person's. They cannot be edited or dismissed.

Since this type of class often draws out some very personal and sensitive recollections and emotions, confidentiality must be expected and maintained. A safe environment in which to express opinions, experiences, and emotions openly and honestly must be guaranteed. Much of the training day is about raising awareness of what "the other" faces on a daily basis and of the institutionalized systems—financial, educational, political—that exist in our society. It's easy to deny what you can't see. A large piece of this particular effort is reigning in White people's urge to internalize the discussion as a personal attack. In almost every class some individuals will loudly complain that they are tired of being attacked as a racist as they proceed to enumerate their list of friends of color and all that they have done with and for them as if this somehow negates the existence of White privilege.

Strong leaders must stop this in its tracks and redirect the conversation back to the issue of institutional racism. The group must look at racism from a much broader perspective and come to grips with how White society, as a whole, benefits from these systems every day, mostly unaware. After this day, participants may continue enjoying their place

---

1 David Adam, *Flame in My Heart: St. Aidan for Today* (Harrisburg, PA: Morehouse Publishing, 1997).

in this system but can no longer claim ignorance of it. It is our hope that the newfound awareness will bring with it some intention of finding ways to encourage change.

An important reiteration is that the day's training is never an end unto itself. It is not something to be checked off on a required "to do" list. There are always more steps forward to be taken and tools to hone to continue the conversation. By accessing many of the resources used throughout the training day, individuals can recreate what they have experienced in class in their home parishes or institutions. Participants are encouraged to share those efforts with the wider community. This, in itself, is inspiring to other churches to be a part of dismantling racism throughout the diocese. To stress the individual as well as the collective work, leaders often share some of their own experiences to demonstrate the difference one person can make. Be the ripple in the pond, so to speak. As with the participants, leaders also bring their own life journey that has shaped and formed their world perspective. This may have resulted in an obstacle to overcome or been a gift of open thinking, but in all cases it is your story and yours alone.

Awareness is a recurring theme during a training class, both in noticing the evidence of White privilege that is often overlooked in day-to-day living and in the acts of racism we witness and choose to ignore.

A few years after being involved in dismantling racism training, I received a firsthand lesson in this on a visit to my husband's parents' home for a 90th birthday party. While preparing food in the kitchen, I could hear a racist conversation happening in the next room. In all honesty, I have to admit this was not the first time I had been witness to such talk. As disgusted as I was by the words, I also struggled with the joyousness of the occasion and considered letting it just slide for now. The struggle lasted about thirty seconds before I admitted to myself that I had no choice but to respond. Let's just say I was overcome by "awareness." Popping my head around the corner, I stopped the conversation by asking, "Say, John, guess what I'm doing in Atlanta now? I'm teaching antiracism classes!" "Really?!" was the only answer he could muster. A short give-and-take ensued and that's when I heard a younger relative, sixteen, join in with the same language the adults had been using. It quickly became evident that my attention needed to focus on this young man. This young person needed to hear another voice—my voice. I may not change the world, but I was able to reveal to this young person another perspective.

Flexibility is critical to this training. Every group has its own personality and good facilitators will recognize it in short order. This is where the importance of a solid relationship between the trainers is evident as they read the group and make subtle changes in their approach to fit the situation. The difference is often seen when the class is composed of individuals predominately from one parish as opposed to an open class comprised of many parishes. While casual conversation comes easily to folks who all know each other, deeper, more substantive conversation can be hampered. Revealing very personal and possibly controversial things about yourself to people you will see tomorrow morning at church can be a bit daunting; it may not be as difficult if the group is composed of individuals you are unlikely to meet again. This is why the tenets of respect and confidentiality are repeated several times during the day. All of this takes elemental faith and trust; the relationships among the trainers and each member of the group is foundational. These topics are tough and intimate, often calling into question long-held beliefs and assumptions. The ability to allow ourselves the opportunity to engage people before making snap judgments is part of the experiential learning this training offers.

Different levels of acceptance are seen in every class. Some participants are shocked and horrified at what they have failed to see and understand. Often, these individuals will decide quickly that they wish to make a difference, returning to their home parish with a new action plan. For this personality, one day of dismantling racism training is not enough and they will look for more opportunities to explore things in more depth.

Others are scared and angry—to face the truth of racism means a whole new life perspective—especially the ones who benefit from the current systems. For these individuals, the training can be excruciating. They may also be the most disruptive and combative. Again, strong leaders are so important. The goal is not to squash them but to facilitate navigation to a new viewpoint, possible only when persons feel heard and respected.

It can be a struggle, at times, for facilitators to keep emotions in check as participants are allowed a safe space to air their opinions or controversial perspectives. I try to channel St. Aidan and meet people where they are. By exhibiting the gift of grace under pressure, we are modeling the behavior being asked of everyone present as well as modeling the sorts of conversations participants may have later with friends and coworkers. Remember, participants are being asked to continue the conversation in the days to come and were promised the training would provide a variety of necessary tools.

While civil rights accomplishments are recognized and celebrated, the reality of the long road ahead must be acknowledged with a commitment to keep putting one foot in front of another always, moving forward.

Catherine

That long road ahead of us is going to be marked over the next three years by a series of memorial martyrdom pilgrimages to sites where lynchings took place. There will be a short memorial liturgy offered by the pilgrims and a marker will be placed at one of the sites, bearing the names of all those who were lynched in that particular city or county. Along with this, book studies, film series, table talks, and other forms of group conversations will be offered to encourage greater knowledge about lynching. We are interested in helping our diocese develop a greater literacy about the intersections among slavery, lynching, mass incarceration, and the death penalty.

The Commission is convinced that its work is to foster education around the issue of race and to become involved as widely as possible through very intentional actions. This may be accomplished by speaking out on certain issues in the community, paying attention to political issues that affect the quality of racial health in our diocese, and any other activities which can support the important work of dismantling racism so that the Beloved Community can come into being. The public support of Bishop Robert Wright of the Diocese of Atlanta for the work the Commission has been given and his personal commitment has been a major force in energizing this endeavor. Bishop Wright's forceful pastoral letter intended to be read in every parish prior to the Repentance and Reconciliation Service was of such significance, as was his presence on each of the Jonathan Daniels Pilgrimages. This type of public declaration of support from him as chief pastor is vitally important in establishing the priority for our work. The Commission meets six times a year, with each meeting beginning with a substantial spiritual formation activity led by different members. We have an annual day-long retreat and are intentional in modeling what we are trying to teach about being the Beloved Community. To reach more of the parishes in the diocese, the 2016 Commission meetings will be held in parishes around the diocese. Additionally, training sessions across the diocese will be hosted by congregations in each convocation.

Many parishes are taking up the challenge of organizing their own conversation groups, screening films, and organizing dismantling racism forums and workshops. Some of them seek counsel from our Commission and many ask for our assistance in the implementation of their programs. The Commission takes delight in the initiatives taken at the parish level to include the topic of race and dismantling racism as a part of the programs for the year.

It is the vision of the Commission to see the Episcopal Diocese of Atlanta approaching dismantling racism as a regular part of the spiritual formation of the parishes with programs designed to support that effort. There will be no need for this body when the work of dismantling racism is properly seen as a part of the ongoing spiritual formation of the family of God. We are holding this vision in our minds and hearts as we continue to forge ahead.

By the time we complete the upcoming three-year cycle of memorial pilgrimages to lynching sites, we hope to have developed a significant body of material to be used for continued study by youth and children as well as adults. This process is a continuation of the current consulting that the Commission has provided in helping middle and high school Sunday school teachers develop their curriculum around racial justice.

The Commission has been called upon nationally by several dioceses to offer counsel and consulting as they have endeavored to expand their work and in a few cases to help their Commission to move their work forward. This has been done through visits to other dioceses and in some cases having members come to Atlanta to participate in some of the scheduled trainings.

Four years ago, we became determined to reinvigorate our work, and that intention has been affirmed in every way by parishes, the new life and energy that we see growing throughout the diocese, and in the overall attitude of many who were not sure that this work was needed. The conversations are expanding as awareness grows about the need for racial healing and it is our great expectation to see this work continue to thrive in the weeks and months to come.

And we also hope to see our diocese bloom as a Beloved Community as we reach across the barriers of race to live into God's Dream. We wish to see our brothers and sisters across the land began to live more fully into God's Dream and we firmly believe that the transformation that we have seen in our work is possible for any and all who are committed to following the racial healing path. It has been a delight to share our story with others who are seeking to reinvigorate their work. Our Commission and others in our diocese stand ready at all times to offer any assistance or encouragement that we can to help any person or group who is reimagining their work or expanding it.

Questions for Individual
or Group Reflection

These questions are designed to be discussed in groups or are appropriate for personal study. Use in ongoing contemplative prayer groups would be especially appropriate because silence can help to heal old wounds and allows for ideas and issues to emerge in ways that discussion without silence cannot.

Beginning the Conversation

Where did you first become aware of race or racial differences? Can you name any of the emotions that you felt at that time? What did you learn about race as a child?

When did you first learn about being (*your race*)? What was the context? How did discovering that you were (*your race*) make you feel?

▌CHAPTER 1

1. "Racism persists because a large segment of the population benefits from it." Reflect upon this statement and list several ways you can see how segments of the population benefit from racism. How much thought have you given to this idea in the past?

2. If the transformation of hearts alone will not undo racism, what will? What other elements are needed to succeed in this challenging work?

3. What are the elements required to inspire our commitment to overcome racism?

4. Reflect upon Thurman's ideas about the way in which differences should be embraced. How do you embrace differences? What helps you to embrace them as you do?

5. What are the greatest challenges that you face in trying to live as a caring neighbor to everyone? How do you work to meet those challenges?

▍CHAPTER 2

1. What were you told about members of different racial or ethnic groups? What kinds of comments were made about members of different racial or ethnic groups in your household? Were there any racial or ethnic slurs or compliments or was yours a household where race wasn't discussed but only hinted at or acted out in innuendo?

2. Where did you learn about race in school—was it from textbooks or teachers and what exactly did you learn? How did this information form your attitudes or feelings about your own ethnic or racial group and those from other racial or ethnic groups?

3. How has your thinking about race changed and what led to the shift?

4. Who are you? What do you know of your identities that comprise your self-concept? What defines you in your daily life? Do you ever move through the day thinking about being _____ (race/gender/social status)?

5. What category (master status) do you focus on when you encounter a stranger? What does this choice of master status suggest about your self-concept?

▌CHAPTER 3

1. Do you have a story about a moment in your life that changes your viewpoint? If so, how did it change you?

2. Why is the idea of race as an illusion a difficult one for Black people to embrace?

3. What is colorblindness and why is it not helpful to people of color?

4. Do you think that people of color and White people can form authentic relationships built on trust, love, and acceptance? Do you have such relationships?

▌CHAPTER 4

1. Why is it dangerous to the human psyche to allow small racists acts, so called microaggressions, go unchecked?

2. Why is it unhealthy to accept negative projections as social constructions? How can a better pattern of choices be established?

3. Is it difficult for you to engage in conversation about race with those outside of your race? Reflect upon the reasons for your experiences or discomfort.

4. Why are the reasons for Black rage just as prevalent today as in the 1960s? What do you think will need to happen in the United States to change this situation?

▌CHAPTER 5

1. What do you think affected the author of this chapter the most as he learned about the reality of race? Think about the moments in your life that helped you to embrace the reality of race.

2. What are some of the conflicts that you have had around issues of social justice and equality?

3. How was Don Mosley influenced by Clarence Jordan? Have you had similar experiences with people who have crossed your path? How did the encounter inform your present outlook on life?

4. "Our greatest reward, whether in distant lands or back home at Jubilee, is the love we share with the beautiful children of this world." Why do you think this is true? Does this statement reflect your view of the world in any way?

▌CHAPTER 6

1. With whom do you talk about racism or White privilege? If you are White, how and when do you talk about these issues when you are with just White friends? Is the conversation different when you are with people of color? If so, why, and how does noticing that difference make you feel?

2. If racism is an exploitative system set up by White people, maintained by White people, and benefiting White people, who has the primary responsibility for dismantling it? If White people have a primary responsibility for dismantling structural racism, what is a primary responsibility for people of color?

3. A preview of the movie *Selma* led to a small group of friends wondering what might happen if every child in America—Black and White—could see this powerful portrayal of a defining moment in our history: How might it strengthen and inspire young people, creating even more energy for racial justice? This wonderful "what if?" question led to 300,000 students getting free tickets to see the movie in theaters across the country, and culminated in every American high school receiving a DVD of the film and a curriculum guide suggesting ways to use it. What "what if?" questions can you think of that hold the seeds of excitement and great change?

▮ CHAPTER 7

1. What interesting coincidences have happened in your life that might have led you to greater congruence between soul and the role that you play in life?

2. When have you been confronted with your own unconscious prejudice? How did you deal with it?

3. What experiences have you had of safe space in groups you worked with? How might these inform your work across lines of human difference in future work you do?

▮ CHAPTER 8

1. What thoughts and feelings are provoked within you when thinking about the American South as the Holy Land?

2. "Facts don't fly high enough or reach deep enough. Poetry riding on melody is necessary," proclaims the author of this chapter as he describes the Holy Land for the United States which is the American South. Why does music help make sense of the comparisons that are being made between the American South and the biblical Holy Land?

3. The author of this chapter argues that the places where God jolts us out of old ways of seeing into new ones can be called holy. How does this idea strike you? When have you been jolted from one place to another? How do you look at that experience? Does it seem holy to you? Why?

4. Both spirituals and the blues are used to illustrate the "Holy Land" quality of the American South. Can you imagine why the folks mentioned in the chapter sang the spirituals and the blues almost interchangeably?

❙ CHAPTER 9

1. This chapter tells the story of the Dismantling Racism Commission in Atlanta. What do you know about the work of dismantling racism which is occurring in your community? Who is charged with doing this work? Have you been involved in doing such work?

2. What do you believe could be the hardest part of having conversations about race such as the ones that you would expect to have in a dismantling racism workshop?

3. Do you find that there are many places in your community where a conversation on race can easily occur? If not, can you imagine yourself helping to facilitate the start of such an endeavor?

4. It seems that the Episcopal Diocese of Atlanta is attempting to make dismantling racism a central place in its work. Do you see that as an option in your church or community?

Suggested Activities to Promote Conversation on Race

1. Invite a small group of your peers who represent your racial group to have a conversation with you about a topic related to dismantling racism and racial healing. After several meetings and when the group feels secure enough, expand the group to include folks of other races.

2. Organize a film study group using films such as *Selma, Crash, Roots,* and *Twelve Years a Slave* to view together and engage in dialogue about.

3. Organize a book study using books that will enlighten all participants about race. You might wish to begin with one of the following or another similar book: *The New Jim Crow, Just Mercy, Between the World and Me,* and *Waking Up White.*

4. Make a personal commitment to read a set number of books related to a racial or ethnic group which is different from yours.

5. Be intentional about going to concerts, plays, and parts of the city in which you live where there is an opportunity for you to engage in conversation with folks who do not have the same ethnic and racial background as you.

6. Encourage your church, social club, homeowners association and others to make sure that all efforts are being made to be inclusive and do whatever you are able to do to raise awareness in these arenas about dismantling racism and racial healing.

Resources

Books

Bolen, Jean Shinoda. *Crossing to Avalon: A Woman's Midlife Pilgrimage.* San Francisco: HarperSanFrancisco, 1994.

Braverman, Mark. *Fatal Embrace: Christians, Jews and the Search for Peace in the Holy Land.* New York: Beaufort Books, 2010.

Forer, Richard. *Breakthrough: Transforming Fear into Compassion—A New Perspective on the Israel-Palestine Conflict.* Albuquerque, NM: Insight Press, 2010.

Huber, Lynn W. *Revelations on the Road: A Pilgrim Journey.* Boulder, CO: Woven Word Press, 2003.

Hwoschinsky, Carol. *Listening with the Heart: A Guide for Compassionate Listening.* 4th edition. Indianola, WA: Compassionate Listening Project, 2006.

Irving, Debby. *Waking Up White, and Finding Myself in the Story of Race.* Chicago: Elephant Room Press, 2014.

Kendrick, Stephen, and Paul Kendrick. *Sarah's Long Walk: The Free Blacks of Boston and How Their Struggle for Equality Changed America.* Boston: Beacon Press, 2004. The little known story of an African American child who started the fight for desegregation in America's public schools that culminated with *Brown v. Board of Education.*

Metta, John. "I, Racist." *Those People.* July 6, 2015. Accessed on January 5, 2016. https://thsppl.com/i-racist-538512462265#.cn36ee9py. Sermon delivered by an African American writer explaining why he never talks about race with his White family and friends.

Palmer, Parker. *Healing the Heart of Democracy: The Courage to Create a Politics Worthy of the Human Spirit.* San Francisco: Jossey-Bass, 2011.

———. *A Hidden Wholeness: The Journey Toward an Undivided Life.* San Francisco: Jossey-Bass, 2004.

Savary, Louis et al. *Dreams and Spiritual Growth: A Judeo-Christian Way of Dreamwork*. Mahwah, NJ: Paulist Press, 1984. Includes thirty-seven specific, detailed methods of doing dream work, with or without a journal.

Shermer, Michael. *The Moral Arc: How Science and Reason Lead Humanity toward Truth, Justice and Freedom*. New York: Henry Holt, 2015.

Online Resources

Center for Courage and Renewal. The Center's mission is to create a more just, compassionate, and healthy world by nurturing personal and professional integrity and the courage to act on it. Parker Palmer's work is the core of this, with a focus on the congruence between soul and role. For more information and resources see www.couragerenewal.org.

Compassionate Listening Project. CLP teaches powerful skills for peacemaking in our families, communities, on the job, and for use in social change work locally and globally. See www.compassionatelistening.org.

National Coalition Building Institute. NCBI does excellent diversity training. See their website for information: www.ncbi.org.

Non-Violent Communication (NVC). Sometimes called Compassionate Communication, this method of conflict resolution was developed by Marshall Rosenberg. For resources, history, and methodology see www.cnvc.org

Racial Healing and Reconciliation Documentary Project. This 2012 documentary produced by Intercultural Productions in collaboration with the Southern Jamaica Plain Health Center, the Boston Public Health Commission, and the Kellogg Foundation is a seventeen-minute glimpse into the practical work of healing from racism through a Boston area community health center's youth initiative. Find online at: www.youtube.com/watch?v=84imro3UVig.

Contributors

Catherine Meeks, PhD, is the retired Clara Carter Acree Distinguished Professor of Socio Cultural Studies from Wesleyan College and founding executive director of the Lane Center for Community Engagement and Service as well as a midwife to the soul of her students and workshop participants. She has spent many years sharing the insights that she gained from her pursuit of the truth. She writes a biweekly column for the *Telegraph* in Macon, is frequently asked to present commentaries on Georgia Public Radio, and is often on local television programs. She is the author of five books and one inspirational CD. Currently she chairs the Beloved Community: Commission for Dismantling Racism for the Episcopal Diocese of Atlanta and brings four decades of experience to the work which has helped her to lead the Commission in transforming the dismantling racism work in Atlanta. She continues to be a sought-after teacher and workshop leader. She holds a Master's Degree in Social Work from Clark Atlanta University and PhD from Emory University.

Luther E. Smith Jr., PhD, is Professor Emeritus of Church and Community at the Candler School of Theology of Emory University. Dr. Smith has written numerous articles and speaks extensively on issues of church and society, congregational renewal, Christian spirituality, and the thought of Howard Thurman. He is the author of *Howard Thurman: The Mystic as Prophet*; *Intimacy and Mission: Intentional Community as Crucible for Radical Discipleship*; editor of *The Pan-Methodist Social Witness Resource Book*; *Howard Thurman: Essential Writings*; coeditor of *The Living Wisdom of Howard Thurman: A Visionary for Our Time* (six compact disc recordings of Howard Thurman's sermons, lectures, and meditations); and senior advisory editor for the five volume *The Papers of Howard Washington Thurman*. He is an ordained minister of the Christian Methodist Episcopal Church. Dr. Smith helped to found the International Community School that has as its mission educational excellence for children who have experienced the traumas of war and violence. He is a cofounder of the Interfaith Children's Movement that educates, mobilizes, and networks faith communities in being advocates for all children.

Lerita Coleman Brown, PhD, is professor of psychology emerita at Agnes Scott College in Decatur, Georgia, where she served as Ayşe I. Carden Distinguished Professor of Psychology and director of the Science Center for Women. Professor Brown, who holds a PhD in social psychology from Harvard University, has published over thirty articles and one edited book on topics ranging from women, work, and aging to stigma, identity, and self-concept. Trained at the Shalem Institute for Spiritual Formation, Professor Brown serves as a spiritual director/companion, leads a "Sistas in Silence" contemplative prayer group, and is an active member of Spiritual Directors International. Her most recent paper, "Praying without Ceasing: Basking in the Loving Presence of God," appeared in Rosalie Norman-McNaney, Sherry Johnson, Therese Taylor-Stinson, eds., *Embodied Spirits: Stories of Spiritual Directors of Color*. Professor Brown writes about contemplative spirituality in everyday life and uncovering the peace in one's heart on her website (peaceforhearts.com).

Don Mosley is a speaker, writer, and organizer who continually promotes peace, justice, and understanding among people around the world. He and his wife, Carolyn, live at Jubilee Partners, a Christian service community in northeast Georgia of which they were cofounders in 1979. Don was a Peace Corps volunteer in Malaysia and a Peace Corps regional director in South Korea. His undergraduate majors were in history, math, and engineering. He has an MA in anthropology. The Mosleys spent the 1970s at Koinonia Farm in southwest Georgia, where Don was the director for several years. During that time he helped launch Habitat for Humanity as a means of overcoming racism and serving homeless people. Don, Carolyn, and the rest of the Jubilee staff have hosted about 4,000 refugees from dozens of countries around the world. This work often draws the Jubilee people into special projects in areas of conflict. The story of how their faith leads them into such actions is told in his books, *With Our Own Eyes* (1996) and *Faith Beyond Borders, Doing Justice in a Dangerous World* (2010). The main goal of the Jubilee community members is to follow Jesus Christ as faithfully as they can through compassionate service to others.

Diane D'Souza has a passion for creating healing spaces that support positive transformation. She currently directs the Mission Institute, a collaborative initiative of the Episcopal Diocese of Massachusetts and the Episcopal Divinity School. She is also the founder and CEO of SWAT Assist, an organization that provides advocacy, intervention, and personal management assistance for elders. Her work has been profoundly shaped by twenty years living in India, where she was a faculty member and director of the Hyderabad-based Henry Martyn Institute, an international center for research, interfaith relations, and reconciliation. While there, she founded a vibrant Conflict Transformation program; developed the Women's Interfaith Journey project that brought together international teams of women to travel and explore female roles in dialogue, conflict, and peacebuilding; taught Islam and Christian-Muslim relations; and conducted research on Muslim women's religious practices. She holds a doctor of philosophy degree in theology from Vrije Universitat in Amsterdam, Netherlands, as well as degrees from McGill University in Montreal, Canada. She has taught courses and conducted workshops in Europe, Asia, Africa, and North America, and is the author of books and publications in the fields of religion, dialogue, peace-building, and social justice.

Lynn W. Huber, MSW, PhD, is a social worker and spiritual director who has both practiced and taught in both fields. She developed and administered the Affirmative Aging program for the Episcopal Diocese of Tennessee. She has offered continuing education courses at the Church Divinity School of the Pacific (Berkeley, California), the University of the South (Sewanee, Tennessee), and the Gerontological Pastoral Care Institute at Luther Seminary in St. Paul, Minnesota. She founded and coordinated the Stillpoint School for Spiritual Development in Little Rock, Arkansas, and was on the faculty for the Benedictine Spiritual Formation Program in Denver and Colorado Springs for several years. Lynn has published a number of articles and her book *Revelations on the Road: A Pilgrim's Journey* (2004) is being used for individual spiritual formation and for small group study in congregations. Lynn offers workshops and retreats as well as spiritual direction for individuals and groups. She is actively involved in prison ministry, and works in peace and justice, especially now in opposing the occupation of Palestine. Lynn is an oblate of Benet Hill Monastery in Colorado Springs, and was the founding convener of the Colorado Chapter of the Episcopal Peace Fellowship.

The Right Rev. Robert Christopher Wright was elected June 2, 2012, by lay delegates and priests of the Diocese of Atlanta to become the 10th bishop in the diocese's 105-year history. He was ordained and consecrated a bishop on Saturday, October 13, 2012, at Martin Luther King Jr. International Chapel on the campus of Morehouse College. He is the first African American to become an Episcopal bishop in Georgia. He earned a Bachelor's Degree from Howard University, a certificate in biblical studies at Ridley Hall, Cambridge University in England, and a master of divinity from the Virginia Theological Seminary, Alexandria, Virginia. As the 10th bishop of the Diocese of Atlanta, he has made a lasting mark regarding the way that the twenty-first-century Christian needs to respond to the call of God. He has joined garbage workers, as well as police officers, both in prayer and going through a shift with them. He is an outspoken death penalty abolitionist who attends as many vigils of protest as possible when executions occur. He joined those delivering signatures to the governor in support of Medicaid expansion and has been a courageous and supportive voice in the work of dismantling racism in the diocese.

Beth King is currently a Dismantling Racism trainer and member of the Beloved Community: Commission for Dismantling Racism in the Episcopal Diocese of Atlanta. A native of North Carolina and graduate of the University of North Carolina at Chapel Hill, her passion for social justice issues was fueled through working with refugees and Hispanic ministries. Having previously served on the diocesan Commission for Spiritual Growth, she now serves as a member of the Standing Committee, The Ministries Innovation Task Force, and a lay missioner and Advisory Board Member for The Church of the Common Ground, a diocesan ministry with the homeless in downtown Atlanta. In addition to work within the diocese, she is a founding member of Women's Interfaith Network (WIN) in Roswell, Georgia. This group of compassionate women seeks to explore and celebrate the commonalities of the Abrahamic faiths while supporting each other in living out their faith traditions in the surrounding cultural context. This is her first published work; her writings of essays and poems have been an important part of her own personal spiritual journey.